Computer Applications for

CONSUMER BEHAVIOR
IN
MARKETING STRATEGY

JOHN A. HOWARD
Graduate School of Business
Columbia University

PRENTICE HALL, Englewood Cliffs, NJ 07632

Editorial/production supervision and
  interior design: Dominic J. Pandiscia
Manufacturing buyer: Margaret Rizzi

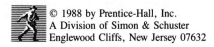

Printed in the United States of America

10 9 8 7 6 5 4 3 2 1

ISBN: 0-13-169731-5

Prentice-Hall International (UK) Limited, *London*
Prentice-Hall of Australia Pty. Limited, *Sydney*
Prentice-Hall Canada Inc., *Toronto*
Prentice-Hall Hispanoamericana, S.A., *Mexico*
Prentice-Hall of India Private Limited, *New Delhi*
Prentice-Hall of Japan, Inc., *Tokyo*
Simon & Schuster Asia Pte. Ltd., *Singapore*
Editora Prentice-Hall do Brasil, Ltda., *Rio de Janeiro*

TABLE OF CONTENTS

041571

Chapter 1

Review of Regression

Computer Applications

for

Consumer Behavior in Marketing Strategy

Chapter Outline

- Introduction

- Dependent and Independent Variables

- Types of Relationships

- Scatter Diagrams

- Correlation Coefficient

- Regression

    - Regression Model

    - Interpretation of b_0 b_1

    - Prediction

    - Multiple Regression

INTRODUCTION*

The purpose of this chapter is to provide a simple overview of regression, a statistical technique commonly used to identify and measure the association or relationship between two or more variables.

While doing this, the chapter provides a description of correlational analysis, the distribution between dependent and independent variables, and the technique of multiple regression.

Dependent and Independent Variables

Consumer researchers often must determine whether there is an association between two or more variables (for example between intention to buy and attitude). And, if present, he/she has to determine the strength and functional form of this relationship. Quite often, we make a distinction between two kinds of variables -- namely, dependent and independent variables. Variables which we try to predict the value of are called the dependent or criterion variables. The variables that are used to predict or explain the dependent variables are called the independent or predictor variables.

Types of Relationships

The relationship or association between any two variables could be either

      a)   linear

or   b)   non-linear

---

* Prepared by Srinivas K. Reddy, New York University

A linear relationship exists between two variables when the value of one variable (Y) increases or decreases by a constant amount with a unit change in the other variable (X) over the entire range of values of this variable (X). If, on the other hand, the value of the variable (Y) changes by a different amount with a unit change of the other variable (X) over different range of values of X, then the relationship is non-linear.

In either of these cases, the relationship is direct or positive if the value of one variable (Y) increases with increasing values of other variable (X). The relationship is considered to be inverse or negative if the value of one variable (Y) increases with decreasing values of the other variable or decreases with increasing values of the other variable.

These are easily demonstrated graphically, as shown in Figures 1 and 2. Figures 1 and 2 demonstrate the linear relationship. The relationship between advertising and sales is positive as increasing

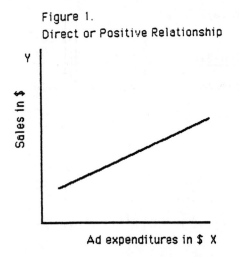

Figure 1.
Direct or Positive Relationship

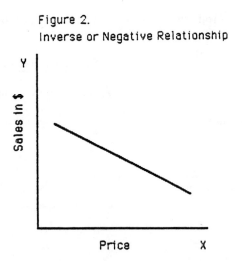

Figure 2.
Inverse or Negative Relationship

advertising expenditures would increase sales. The relationship here
is considered linear, at least within certain range of advertising.
(Though there could be diminishing returns at very high levels of
advertising making the relationship non-linear.)

The relationship between Price and Sales is negative as increasing
prices would diminish sales and it is considered to be linear.

Figures 3 and 4 illustrate the curvilinear relationships.

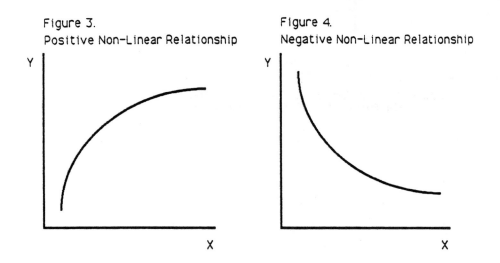

Figure 3.
Positive Non-Linear Relationship

Figure 4.
Negative Non-Linear Relationship

Scatter Diagrams

One of the simpler ways of obtaining a visual clue about the type
of relationship between variables is using scatter diagrams. A scatter
diagram is simply a plot of the values of the variables X and Y on a
two dimensional plane. Such a visual representation of data provides
us with the following kind of information:

a)   is there a relationship between X and Y

5

b) if there is, is the relationship linear or non-linear, positive or negative?

c) is the relationship strong or weak?

Take the following example of data for several MBA students on their GMAT scores and their cumulative GPA. We would like to determine if there is any relationship between student's performance on an entrance test and his performance in the MBA program. The following table shows the data for eight MBA students.

Table 1

Students' Scores on GMAT and Their Cumulative
Grade Point Average in the MBA Program

Student	GMAT Score	Cumulative GPA
1	592	2.6
2	552	2.2
3	680	3.4
4	504	2.3
5	656	3.1
7	632	3.2
8	728	3.8

Plotting the data with the GMAT Scores on the X-axis and the cumulative GPA on the Y-axis will give us a scatter diagram as in Figure 5.

The scatter diagram indicates a positive relationship between the GMAT scores and the cumulative GPA suggesting that if a student does well on the GMAT, he is likely to do well in the MBA program. The plot also suggests that the relationship is linear. As the data points appear to be fairly tight around the straight line, there is indication that the relationship is fairly strong.

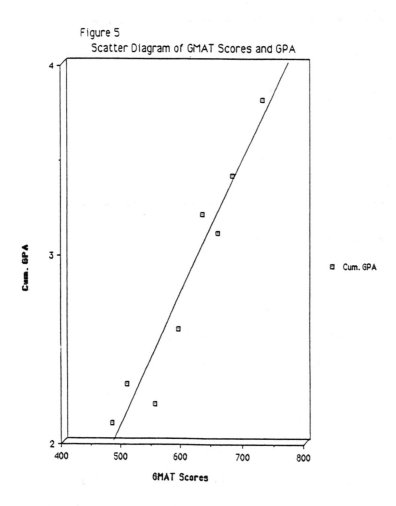

Figure 5
Scatter Diagram of GMAT Scores and GPA

Figure 6 depicts various scatter plots and the associated interpretation of the type of relationship.

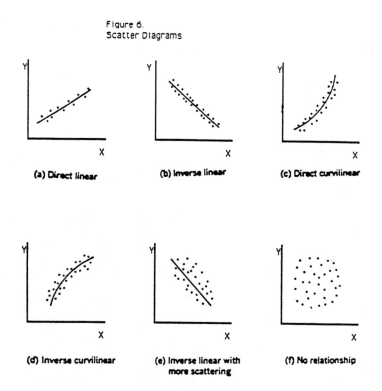

Figure 6.
Scatter Diagrams

(a) Direct linear

(b) Inverse linear

(c) Direct curvilinear

(d) Inverse curvilinear

(e) Inverse linear with more scattering

(f) No relationship

Correlation Coefficient

Though the scatter diagrams shown do suggest the type and strength of relationships, it would be more useful to the investigator to have a tool which quantifies these relationships. There is such a tool available. It is a statistic called correlation or correlation coefficient. It measures the strength and direction of the linear relationship between two variables, and is commonly denoted as 'r.'

The range of values that 'r' can take is from -1 to +1 including the value of zero. The value of 'r' would indicate the strength and direction of the relationship between the two variables. A value closer to 1 indicates a very strong relationship and a positive or a negative sign indicates if the relationship is positive or negative. Figure 7 depicts various scatter diagrams and their resulting correlation coefficients. A careful examination of these diagrams will provide a linkage between the degree of scatter and the correlation coefficient.

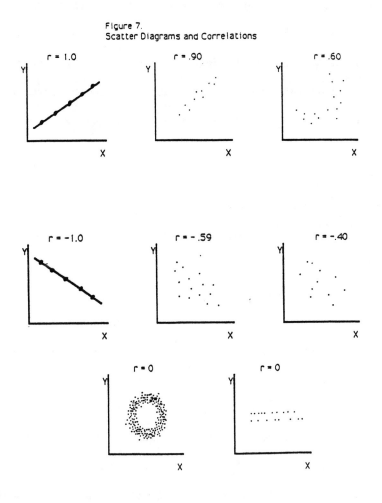

Figure 7.
Scatter Diagrams and Correlations

Regression

Regression Model

Regression analysis is a technique which involves the specification of a dependent variable and which is predicted or explained by a certain number of independent variables. The approach taken in this section is non-technical with greater emphasis on inputs for the model, the output of the model, and their interpretation.

The first step in the construction of a regression model is the specification of the dependent variable and the independent variable or variables. If our purpose is to determine the impact of attitude towards our brand on intention to buy that brand (both measured on, say, a 7-point scale), we may propose the following regression model:

$$Y = b_0, + b_1X + e$$

where

Y = Intention to buy score

X = Attitude towards the brand

e = error term

b_0, b_1 = model parameters.

The above model with just one independent variable X is usually referred to as a "simple regression model." The model parameters b_0 and b_1 characterize the relationship between X and Y. If we can gather data from several consumers on their attitude and intention to buy our brand, we could then determine what the values of b_0 and b_1 are.

If we plot the values of X and Y we get a scatter diagram. The idea now is to obtain a line through these data points which best 'fits' the data. This is usually called the "regression line." Finding

this best fitting line is usually done by means of a computer program.
Let us suppose the following are the estimates obtained from such a
regression line:

$$Y = \hat{b}_0 + \hat{b}_1 X = 2 + 0.2X$$

Notice that the model parameters are now denoted with a $\hat{}$ (hat). This
indicates that they are estimates of b_0 and b_1 obtained from the
sample. The valued estimated for b_0 and b_1 are 2 and 0.2 respectively.

Interpretation of b_0 and b_1

b_0 is called the intercept and is interpreted as the value that Y
would have if the value of X were zero. In the present case, it is the
average of intention to buy among the consumers if their value of
attitude were zero.

b_1 is usually called the slope of the regression line. It
represents the change in Y with a unit change in X. If X is changed by
one unit, the variable Y will change by b_1 units. It suggests the
amount of change in intention to buy that could be expected for every
unit of change in the attitude. The estimate of b_1 is 0.2 indicating
that the relationship is positive and that for every point increase in
attitude, there would be a 0.2 unit increase in intention to buy.

As $\hat{b}_0$ and $\hat{b}_1$ are the estimates of b_0 and b_1 obtained from a sample
one has to wonder how closely they represent the true values of b_0 and
b_1 which exist in the population. If the value of b_1 were zero in the
population, this implies that there is no effect of attitude on intention. As we obtained an estimate of b_1 to be 0.2, one has to question
whether this value which is different from zero is due to sampling

11

error. We need to know if this estimate is significantly different form zero. To test for this one needs to have the standard error (S_{b1}) associated with $\hat{b}_1$ which is also provided by the computer program. We can now construct a t-test to test for the hypothesis that b_1 is zero.

$$t = \hat{b}_1/S_{b1}$$

If the ratio of $\hat{b}_1$ and its standard error S_{b1}, is high (over 2.0) then we reject the hypothesis that b_1 is zero, implying that X does impact Y. If, however, the t-value is small, then we have to conclude that b_1 is in fact zero. This implies that X does not affect Y.

In our example the standard error of $\hat{b}_1$ is 0.05. The t-value then is

$$t = \hat{b}_1/S_{b1} = 0.2/0.05 = 4.0$$

This high t-value implies that b_1 is non-zero, and attitude does impact intention to buy positively.

Prediction

The purpose of regression is not only to extract the effects of independent variable or variables on the dependent variable, but also to predict the value of the dependent variable. Whereas $\hat{b}_1$ is an estimate of the extent of the effect of X on Y, we can obtain an estimate of the predictive power of the independent variable or variables. This estimate, called "r^2" or coefficient of determination, is a measure of how well the independent variables predict the dependent variable.

The estimate of the coefficient of determination is also provided by the computer program. The value of r^2 could range from zero to one. The closer the value of r^2 is to one, the better the predictive power. The interpretation of an r^2 having a value of .7 is that the model explains 70% of the variation in the dependent variable. Though in most instances this is a reasonably good model, there may be other independent variables that could explain the remaining portion of the variation of the dependent variable.

In our example, the r^2 is 0.4. This means that attitude towards the brand explains about 40% of the variation of consumers' intention to buy. This is very good for one independent variable. As we know, there are several other variables which explain intention to buy. And, if those are included, the r^2 may be higher.

Multiple Regression

As we discussed in the previous section, the prediction of the dependent variable is usually not very good if we use just one independent variable. Including more variables will improve the explained variation of the dependent variable and also will provide us information on the relationships of other independent variables with the dependent variable.

If we were to include other variables to impact intention to buy, we would improve the prediction. We selected knowledge of the brand and comprehension about the brand as the two variables which may have some impact on intention to buy. We can now write this model as

$$Y = b_0 + b_1 X_1 + b_2 X_2 + b_3 X_3 + e$$

13

where Y and X_1 are as defined before

X_2 = knowledge about the brand

X_3 = comprehension about the brand

A model with more than one independent variable is usually referred to as a multiple regression model. If we obtain data from a sample of consumers on all the four variables, we can estimate the four model parameters (b_0, b_1, b_2, b_3) using a computer program. The computer program would not only estimate the parameters but also would provide the associated standard error. Table 2 shows the estimates, the standard errors, and the t-values.

Table 2

Regression Coefficients of the Intention Model

Variable	Parameter	Parameter Estimate	Standard Error $S_b 1$	t×value b_i/S_{bi}
Intercept	b_0	$\hat{b}_0 = 1.2$	0.95	1.26
Attitude (X_1)	b_1	$\hat{b}_1 = 0.16$	0.06	2.67
Knowledge (X_2)	b_2	$\hat{b}_2 = 0.12$	0.05	2.40
Comprehension (X_3)	b_3	$\hat{b}_3 = 0.05$	0.07	0.71

R-square = 0.52

The interpretation of the regression coefficient in the case of multiple regression model is very similar to that of the interpretation in the simple regression with one key difference. For example, the coefficient b_1 is interpreted as the change in the dependent variable Y

14

that would be expected if X_1 increased by one unit, and all other independent variables (X_2 and X_3) remained unchanged.

In our example, $\hat{b}_1 = 0.16$. This can be interpreted as follows: Intention to buy would increase by .16 units if the attitude toward the brand increased by one unit, provided that the knowledge and comprehension remained the same. Similar interpretation can be applied to the other coefficients that are determined to be significantly different from zero.

To check whether the coefficients are significantly different from zero, one has to examine the column that contains the t-values. The coefficients with t-values greater than 2.0 can be considered to have a significant impact on the dependent variable. Attitude and knowledge appear to have a significant positive impact on intention to buy, but comprehension failed to have a significant effect as t-value of 0.71 would suggest.

In our example, we assume that all the variables used in the regression equation are measured on the same scale (for example, on a 7-point scale). This may not be the case in all situations. Some variables could be measured in millions of dollars (like advertising expenditures) and some other things in just dollars (like the price of the product). When these variables are used in a regression equation to predict sales (which is measured in millions of dollars), the regression coefficients associated with each of them would reflect the scale of measurement. The estimates could be as follows:

$$sales = 2.5 + .15 \text{ (advertising)} - 1.2 \text{ (price)}$$

The interpretation of these coefficients is still the same as before.

One may be tempted to conclude that price is a more important variable than advertising because of the absolute size of the coefficient. As the two variables are measured in different units, the magnitudes of these coefficients are not really comparable unless they are transformed somehow to the same scale. This process is called "standardization." Each coefficient is multiplied by the ratio of the standard deviation of the respective independent variable and the standard deviation of the dependent variable. The resulting coefficients are referred to as standardized coefficients or beta (β) coefficients. These coefficients can now be compared to identify which variable has the greatest impact on the dependent variable.

The interpretation of the r^2 is the same in the case of multiple regression. The r^2 for the multiple regression model is 0.52, which is an improvement over the simple regression model that had an r^2 of 0.4. This means that 52% of the variance of intention to buy is explained by the model.

Chapter 2 Quick'n Easy I

Computer Applications

for

Consumer Behavior in Marketing Strategy

Chapter Outline

I	Introduction
II	The IBM 4341 Computer using SAS
III	Use of Other Computing Systems and statistical software
IV	Logging onto the IBM 4341 using SAS
V	Fitting the CDM to the RCA Videodisk Data
VI	Procedure to complete the CDM
VII	Conclusions

I. Introduction

The purpose of "Quick'n Easy" Computer Applications I is to help you learn, quickly and easily, how to model consumer buying.

You have already become familiar with the Customer Decision Model (CDM). Here you will learn how to apply the CDM to actual data, the RCA Videodisk Case. Having gone through this exercise, you can then on your own, using Quick'n Easy II that follows, model each of the three other cases, beginning with Lean Strips.

1. Lean Strips (an innovative vegetable bacon introduced by General Foods in Ft. Wayne, Indiana in 1974)

2. Vega (a subcompact car introduced by General Motors in 1970)

3. Central Asset Accounts case (a study of buyers of cash/asset accounts and particularly Merrill Lynch (Cash Management Account), Dean Witter (Active Asset Account), Shearson (Financial Management Account) and Citibank (Focus Account), in 1985.

---

*By John A. Howard and John Stephan, Columbia University, we thank Sally Strickholm and Robert Coletti for their splendid contributions.

I. Introduction

This is an introductory manual to using SAS programming. Although
the software package is not interactive, it is quite easy to master the
modest amount of SAS** programming needed to model consumer buying
using the CDM. As with any introductory document, only the very basics
are discussed. There is a vast amount of SAS programming available and
many more sophisticated procedures which can be performed. However,
this manual does provide all the information that is required to
complete this assignment, the RCA Videodisk Case.

For the beginner, the prospect of working with a mainframe computer in a programming language can be intimidating. However, let us
assure you that the IBM 4341 computer at the Columbia Business School
with its VM/CMS operating system is quite manageable. The VM (Virtual
Machine) operating system controls the physical devices (such as the
computer tape, disc drives, and the central processing unit (CPU), and
interfaces with various programming languages (e.g., SAS)) which direct
the activity of the computer. It also provides a friendly command-
driven interface for instructing the computer to perform various
tasks. CMS (conversational monitor system) refers to the computer's
main operating system.

**SAS is an acronym for Statistical Analysis System but it
has broadened into an all-purpose data analysis system.

What is needed is an understanding of the work flow of a typical computer session which we have provided below. If you comprehend and remember this flow, your computer sessions will be much more organized, better understood, efficient, and pleasant.

This flow is a typical sequence of events in a computer session for modeling consumer behavior:

1) Log onto the computer

2) Copy the SAS program you need to use from the D disk (data file) to the A disk (working file) with the COPY command

3) Enter the list of files (SAS programs and other files)

4) Enter a desired SAS program using the Executive Editor

5) Modify the program

6) Save changes and exit the program

7) Exit the list of files

8) Run the modified SAS program

9) Enter the list of files again

10) Look at the SAS output file

11) Print the output file

12) Log off (You may repeat steps 3-11 many times before logging off. However, do not forget to log off.)

To the extent that you become familiar with these steps in doing the RCA case, the other cases will be much easier as you will see in Chapter 3 Quick'n Easy II.

This manual obviously provides information on "what to do's," not "how to do's." However, after reading the remainder of this manual you will learn how to actually do each of the above steps. If, during a computer session, you remember what you should be doing, you will most likely remember how to do it and if not, it will be easy for you to look it up. Refer to these 12 basic steps when first working with the computer until you have become familiar with the routine. It will save you a great deal of agony. Good luck and have fun with the course!

III. Use of Other Computing Systems and Statistical Software

Ignore this section if you are using IBM 4341 with SAS software.

The prodecures presented in Quick'n Easy I and II will refer, quite specifically, to using the SAS system on an IBM 4341 computer system running the CMS operating system. While this type of configuration is increasingly popular, it is not the only system that you might encounter when performing statistical analysis. In addition, SAS itself has a number of competitors on both mainframes and personal computers. The procedures and idiosyncrasies of whatever system and software you have available will need to be learned to accomplish the goals of this introduction: learning the use of statistical software to perform analysis (specifically those related to assessing consumer behavior) on data using a computer system.

Although it is true that each computer system and each statistical analysis software package is different from the others, there is a degree of similarity between them that can be used to effectively assimilate the process on one configuration and transfer that process, with minimal difficulty, to another configuration. To this end an outline of such similarities follows.

Mainframe Systems

If you are using a mainframe computer system (rather than a

personal computer), you will need a **computer** ID and **password** and, if you are planning to use a telephone modem, the **telephone number of the computer** in order to gain access to the system. When using a mainframe system, you can use either a terminal or a personal computer to communicate with the mainframe. If you are using a PC, you will also need a communication software package. This allows your PC to behave like a terminal. Popular communication packages are Smartcom, Crosstalk, and Kermit.

With these pieces of information, you log into the computer. The actual log on procedure differs from system to system, but you will be typing both your computer ID and password to gain access. Using a PC, you must start up your communications software, specify what kind of terminal you want the PC to look like, and instruct the software to begin communications. (If you are using a modem, at this time you would dial the phone.) With a terminal, it is usually only necessary to turn it on. You would then dial the phone if you are using a modem. Once you have attracted the mainframe's attention, (by pressing return or some special keystroke combination such as control-numlock and return) you will be asked, in some fashion, for your ID and password.

Once logged in, you now must address the issue of the type of statistical software you have available. These fall into two basic types:

1) Interactive
2) Batch

Interactive software allows you to have a dialogue with the computer. You give a command to the computer, it performs the operation, returns some results to the screen, and then waits for the next command. Batch software necessitates writing a program in the language of the statistical software, that you then ask the software to execute for you. Everything that you want the statistical package to do for you must be included in this program (in the proper order) along with any computer-specific information that the software might need.

If you have an interactive package available (some commercially available ones are SCSS, IDA, PEC, SAS (with FSP)), you will be able to enter both data and program lines interactively, right from the keyboard. However, with larger amounts of data, it is often better to use a text editor and enter the data into an external (to the statistical software) file and then ask the statistical software to read this file. This way, if data entry errors have been made, they will be easily correctable without retyping the entire dataset. It is less necessary to learn a text editor (such as XEDIT, discussed later) with an interactive statistical analysis system, because data entry routines are becoming increasingly robust and have the ability to trap errors and allow you to correct them without losing correctly entered data. With respect to the procedures outlines in Quick'n Easy I and II, the datasets have been provided for you.

To operate the interactive package, you need to know the list of commands the package understands and the command to start up the package. If a given command needs extra information, you will usually be prompted for it by the package. Once in the statistical package, you can follow the same outline presented here:

1) Enter data, if necessary, or tell the statistical package to read your external datafile.

2) Decide what statistical routines to do.

3) Instruct the package to perform these routines. Provide other information when requested by the package.

4) Analyze the results.

5) Instruct the package to perform subsequent analyses.

You will need to know the syntax of the various commands your package understands to perform the statistical procedures discussed in in these guides: regression, clustering, analysis of variance, correlation, etc. Note that some statistical packages do not provide all possible statistical routines.

With a batch statistical system, you would proceed very much as described in the following guides, Quick'n Easy I and II. (SAS, SPSSX, TSP, RATS, etc. are examples of commercially available batch statistical packages.)

1) Use a text editor to create and modify your statistical program. Save the program.

2) Use a text editor to enter your data. Save the data.

3) Ask the statistical package to run (execute) your program.

4) Look at the results.

5) Modify the program to perform different statistical procedures, save it, rerun it, look at results, and so forth.

In some cases, it may be necessary to wait for a printed copy of the results before you can look at them (the system may automatically print output from programs). In others, like SAS using CMS, described in the pages that follow, output files are produced that you may look at before deciding if you want them printed.

Using a batch program requires that you learn a text editor, learn the syntax of the language of the statistical package, and learn the commands necessary for sending your program off to be executed by the statistical system you are using. This final step may simply be a command given at the terminal. It may involve JCL (job control language) included in your program to call up the statistical system, locate datafiles and produce output. Or it may be some combination of these options.

The final consideration in both the interactive and batch packages is understanding the operating system of your computing system so that you can manage the files you will be creating. All operating systems have commands to create and modify files (usually with an editor). Commands to look at the directory of files, COPY, RENAME, ERASE, and PRINT files are also available. You need to become familiar with the syntax of these commands on your system so that you can perform them correctly.

Personal Computer (PC) Systems

If you are using a PC to perform your analysis, the process is not very different from that for mainframe environment. A PC's statistical packages come in three varieties:

1)   Interactive programs.

2)   Menu-driven programs

3)   Batch programs

Interactive and batch programs perform very much like their mainframe counterparts. Interactive programs allow you to have a dialogue with the PC. Once you start up the PC (boot it with the operating system diskette), you then load the statistical software. This entails either inserting the software diskette and issuing a command to start it up, or if you have a hard-disk system, giving the correct command to begin the package. The steps then become very similar to the processes we have been describing. You need to know the commands your statistical package understands for performing the analyses you desire. There are many statistical packages available for PCs. Some are: Statgraphics, Exec*U*Stat, Systat, PC/SAS, SPSSX-PC, NCSS.

1) Once the package begins, you can enter your data or ask the package to read an external file.

2) Issue commands to perform analysis on your data. Output is either directed to your monitor (the screen) or sent to the printer connected to the PC.

3) Examine the output.

4) Request more analysis.

Note that with an interactive package, if you make an error with any command, the software immediately tells you this and you can reissue the command correctly.

A batch-oriented statistical package functions much like a batch oriented package on a mainframe. You use an editor to create your program, written in the language of the statistical package, which will tell the package what analyses to do, on which dataset, etc. You then tell the statistical package to execute this file. Results are, again, directed either to the screen or to the printer. It is obvious that with batch-oriented packages, you must also become familiar with a text editor, in addition to understanding the syntax of the statistical package's commands. Your editor must be capable of producing what are called "standard ASCII files', or non-document files. That is, the programs you create cannot contain any of the editor's underlining, boldfacing, margin setting, or other special characters. Statistical packages cannot understand these special characters.

Finally, menu-driven programs are much like interactive programs. You have a dialogue with the computer, but with a menu system, the things you can do at any time are only those available on the menu you are currently looking at. Once you make a menu selection, you will either see a subsequent menu (necessitating another choice), or you will be asked for other information (e.g., select a variable).

1) You start up the statistical package. You will see some sort of "MAIN MENU."

2) From this main menu, you choose the option to enter data. Then either enter your data from the keyboard, or instruct the package to read your file of data.

3) Then proceed to the menus for data analysis. Select the analyses that you wish to perform. Provide additional information as requested.

4) Examine the results (displayed either on your screen or printed on the printer).

5) Run other analyses. Examine results, and so forth.

Using a PC requires that you have some familiarity with the operating system of the PC. DOS (Disk Operating System) is one of the most popular. You should become familiar with the methods for creating and modifying files (usually with an editor). In addition, command procedures for COPY, ERASE, RENAME, PRINT, and other functions are also useful to manage the files you create using the statistical package.

With all of this said, the process we will describe in the following pages still pertains, no matter what kind of system or what kind of software you will be using. The actual commands you will give to perform each step of the process will differ, but the logic of the steps themselves will be very similar.

IV. Logging onto the IBM 4341 using SAS

The log on procedure is very straightforward. It is slightly different depending on whether you are working in the Business School Computer Lab or dialing in from a remote location.

WORKING AT THE BUSINESS SCHOOL: You need to check out a Y-term diskette from the computer attendant. Place the disk in the A drive of your PC and either turn the machine on or re-boot. (To re-boot, hit the delete key while holding down the Ctrl and Alt keys.)

    Note: YOU NEED TO USE A PC THAT HAS A RED DOT ON THE SIDE OF THE TERMINAL. BLUE DOT TERMINALS DO NOT CONNECT TO THE MAINFRAME.

FROM A REMOTE LOCATION: Place the Y-TERM disk in the A drive of your PC and either turn on the machine or re-boot. You will also need to use a modem to connect to the computer through a telephone line. Instructions will be given on using the modem.

The top half of subsequent pages provides the computer screens that you will encounter during the log on procedure. Supplemental instructions are provided on the bottom half of the page below each screen where needed. Turn the page to see the first screen where you can proceed with logging onto the 4341.

```
+----------------------------------------------------------+
|              Columbia Business School                    |
|            James L. Dohr  Computer Center                |
|         Yterm Version 1.2    April 8, 1985               |
+----------------------------------------------------------+
```

Current date is Tue 1-01-1980
Enter new date (mm-dd-yy):
Current time is 0:00:16.47
Enter new time:

Simply press the enter key(←┘)for each of the two queries -
date and time - since there is no need to enter the date and
time unless you wish to keep a record for future use.

```
Starting Yterm Program...
┌─────────────────────────────────────────────────────────────┐
│        If dialing in, tell Yale ASCII the terminal type is  IBMPC │
│                 To switch color on hit  keypad 5 d           │
│                 To make tab key work hit  keypad 5 c         │
│        Hit  Ctrl-Break  to exit to DOS after logging off.    │
│                 To re-start YTERM type  t 9                  │
└─────────────────────────────────────────────────────────────┘
Strike a key when ready . . .
```

If at any time you should wish to make a copy of a particular
screen being shown, merely turn on your printer and press shift
(⇧) and Prt-Sc simultaneously.

Follow the computer instructions of striking a key (any key)
when you are ready to proceed. Then, if using a modem, call in
to mainframe (212-280-8763). Then to move to the next page,
hit the control (CNTL) key and while holding it down, strike
the NUM LOCK or G (if modeming in) key. Hit "enter."

```
COLUMBIA BUSINESS SCHOOL - DOHR COMPUTER CENTER
Services Available : IBM4341 or IBM3705
SERVICE? ibm4341
WELCOME TO CUGSBVM !
CONNECTED

ENTER TERMINAL TYPE: ibmpc




DISCON      (C) Copyright 1983,1984 Yale University, All Rights Reserved.
```

In response to "SERVICE?," type in IBM4341 and press the "enter" key.

WHEN ASKED for your terminal type, type IBMPC and press the "enter" key. You will see the screen on the following page.

```
GGGGGGG
GGGGGGGGG  $$$$$$$
GG     GG $$$$$$$$$$ BBBBBBBB
GG          $$     $$ BBBBBBBBB
GG          $$        BB    BB
GG    GGGG $$$$$$$$$ BB    BB
GG    GGGG  $$$$$$$$$ BBBBBBB                VM/SP
GG     GG         $$ BBBBBBB                4.0
GGGGGGGGG $$     $$ BB     BB
 GGGGGGG  $$$$$$$$$ BB     BB
         $$$$$$$  BBBBBBBBB
                  BBBBBBBB
```

Columbia Business School
James L. Dohr Computer Center
Network Node: CUGSBVM

                                              RUNNING   CUGSBVM

Press the "enter" key to continue.

Enter one of the following commands:

```
LOGON userid            (Example:  LOGON VMUSER1)
DIAL userid             (Example:  DIAL VMUSER2)
MSG userid message      (Example:  MSG VMUSER2 GOOD MORNING)
LOGOFF
```

			CP READ CUGSBVM
	LOGON	Userid	
	Dial	Userid	
Ignore above message types	MSG	Userid message	
	LOGOFF		

As long as CP READ is showing in the lower right hand corner of your screen above you are ready to log on.

To log on simply type L and the name of the account that has been assigned to you. Press ENTER.

These are our eight class accounts which must be shared:

```
L B860101A
"    "    B
"    "    C
"    "    D
"    "    E
"    "    F
"    "    G
"    "    H
```

```
Enter one of the following commands:

    LOGON userid          (Example:  LOGON VMUSER1)
    DIAL userid           (Example:  DIAL VMUSER2)
    MSG userid message    (Example:  MSG VMUSER2 GOOD MORNING)
    LOGOFF

L B860101A
ENTER PASSWORD  (IT WILL NOT APPEAR WHEN TYPED):




                                                    CP READ    CUGSBVM
```

Type in the password.

If you notice in the upper left corner (above), you have logged
onto the A account. Just type in the password and press the
"enter" key. The screen will fill up with system-related
messages, and you may notice in the lower right corner of the
screen the word MORE.... Whenever you encounter this signal
you must press the "+" key on the far right side of the keyboard which is the CLEAR key. This will allow the next screen
to be displayed.

Important: Sometimes "MORE" in lower right does not appear at
this exact point if the messages are too voluminous. If it
doesn't appear, it will probably appear later, and when it
does, use the above command of press "+" key on the far right
side of the keyboard.

```
*
* Simscript II.5 now available.  Invoke with SIMSCRPT command.
*
* =======================================================================
LOGON AT 15:14:01 EST TUESDAY 03/24/87
VM/SP REL 4 05/01/86 16:58
```

```
                                                    VM READ    CUGSBVM
```

Press the "enter" key to continue when you see: "VM/SP REL 4..."

V. Fitting the CDM to the RCA Videodisk Data

You are now fully logged on to the 4341 computer and you are ready to proceed with fitting the model to the data. Go ahead, moving from screen to screen just as you have been, but you will soon begin to see evidence that you are really dealing with consumers and their interest in the videodisk.

```
*
* Simscript II.5 now available.  Invoke with SIMSCRPT command.
*
* ====================================================================
LOGON AT 15:14:01 EST TUESDAY 03/24/87
VM/SP REL 4 05/01/86 16:58


D (192) R/O
DMSACC113S 'B (193) ' NOT ATTACHED
R; T=0.02/0.03 15:15:13
```

The R; T=0.01/0.01 is your CMS ready prompt. You need to have
this signal in order to execute the various system commands you
will become familiar with. You now want to build your own file
to work with. Since you have now received the CMS ready prompt
signal (R; T=0.01/0.01) you type

        COPY RCAINPT SAS A _____ SAS A (REPLACE)

filling the blank with any eight letter word of your
own choosing, that will uniquely identify the program you are
copying from the RCAINPT SAS A file on to a file in your own
A-disk on the mainframe.

Press "enter" which will give screen with cap "R" as you see
above somewhere on screen if there is no error. If an error
occurs, there will be a number in addition to the R;. The
number is not explanatory, however. If this occurs, try
reissuing the command.

What you have copied is the beginning of a SAS program. You
will be adding various procedures to your file as you go along.
The reason for having a unique file name is that other people
may be using the same account number that you are using. Be sure not
to forget the name that you have given your file because you
will be asked to type it again later.

Hit F10 to get to a list of the files and F9 to have the files
in the right order (by date).

```
   LVL.0 ── A 191      900 BLKS 3375 R/W      8 FILES  4% ── FILE      1 OF      8
HOLDNESS  SAS       A1 __                 F    80    16    2  3/24/87 15:17
HOLDNESS  LISTING   A1                    V    76    45    2  3/10/87 17:36
HOLDNESS  SASLOG    A1                    V    90    26    2  3/10/87 17:36
GENERAL   SAS       A1                    F    80    20    2 12/02/86  9:48
VEGAAGGI  SAS       A1                    F    80    45    4 11/29/86 14:44
MAVRICK   SAS       A1                    F    80    42    4 11/21/86 15:02
WAGON     SAS       A1                    F    80    35    3 11/21/86 12:16
PROFILE   EXEC      A2                    V    23     8    1  9/30/86 12:22
```

Each student account has on it a file called "Profile Exec."
It is essential because it sets up the F10 key to display the
list of files and also links other disks. Do not erase "Profile Exec" if you should be clearing your files.

Place the cursor at the file _____ SAS A1 (that you created
with the COPY command) and press the key F4. This enables you
to use the Executive Editor, XEDIT, to modify this file in any
way that you wish. This causes the next screen to appear.

Once you are in XEDIT, as you will be on the next screen,
if you wish to log off, you must first get out of XEDIT back
into VM/CMS. To do this press F3 twice and type "LogOff" and
press enter. (You will disconnect from the computer.)

```
HOLDNESS SAS        A1  F 80  Trunc=80 Size=16 Line=0 Col=1 Alt=0

=====  * * * Top of File * * *
       !...+....1....+....2....+....3....+....4....+....5....+....6....+....7..
=====  OPTIONS PS = 60 LS = 80;
=====
=====  CMS FI GREEN DISK RCA DAT D;
=====
=====  DATA;
=====  INFILE GREEN;
=====  INPUT P_VD 1 P_RCA 2 I_PAST 3 I_FUTR 4 C 5
=====  A_PRICE 6 A_FEATR 7 A_NAME 8 A_MOVIE 9 B_PRICE 10
=====  B_FEATR 11 B_STOP 12 B_RECRD 13 B_RPRICE 14
=====  W_PRICE 15 W_FEATR 16 W_NAME 17 W_MOVIE 18
=====  F_FRND 19 F_TV 20 F_TVAD 21 F_SVC 22 F_CHLD 23
=====  F_CR 24 F_MAGZN 25 I_RCA 26;
=====  WA_FEATR = A_FEATR * W_FEATR;
=====  WA_NAME = A_NAME * W_NAME;
=====  F = F_CR + F_CHLD + F_TVAD;
=====  PROC REG SIMPLE; MODEL WA_FEATR = F /STB;
=====  * * * End of File * * *

====>
                                              X E D I T  1 File
```

According to the information on this screen what step or
portion of a step in the modeling of the RCA videodisk are you
now attempting to accomplish? You now are doing Step 5.

Since we are not going to change the program at this time,
press F3 twice (allow a moment between the two presses) to exit
the editor and the file directory (file list) which will take
you to the next page.

Now you are ready to run the regression program you copied and looked at on the previous page.

Type SAS _____ (your file name) and hit "enter" key. The regression program proceeds to run.

Errors in SAS Program

As the regression program runs you may see references to errors. You may have left out a "t," typed in an incorrect symbol, or any one of a number of other things.

If you notice errors, press F10 and F9 to check the SASLOG, which is designed for dealing with errors, by putting the cursor on _____ (your file name) SASLOG and pressing F2 to

browse the file. Look through the pages referred to in the
SASLOG message until the error message is found. Then figure
out the correction needed and press F3 to get out of browse and
return to the list of files. Then move the cursor to _____
(your file name) SAS and press F4 to Xedit and make corrections
needed. Press "enter" once the changes are made, type "file"
(to SAVE the changes) and press "enter" again and rerun the
program.

```
SAS VERSION 5.08 COLUMBIA BUSINESS SCHOOL
------------------------------------------

Running HOLDNESS SAS ...

Job Completed.
R; T=1.00/2.21 15:20:01
```

RUNNING   CUGSBVM

Here you notice that SAS has completed the run of your program.
If you will press F10 (file list) and F9 (so that the files are
listed with the most recent file first), you will get the next
page.

```
   LVL 0 —— A 191    900 BLKS 3375 R/W    8 FILES  4% —— FILE      1 OF      8
   HOLDNESS SASLOG    A1                   V    90    25    2  3/24/87 15:20
   HOLDNESS LISTING   A1 __                V    76    45    2  3/24/87 15:20
   HOLDNESS SAS       A1                   F    80    16    2  3/24/87 15:17
   GENERAL  SAS       A1                   F    80    20    2 12/02/86  9:48
   VEGAAGGI SAS       A1                   F    80    45    4 11/29/86 14:44
   MAVRICK  SAS       A1                   F    80    42    4 11/21/86 15:02
   WAGON    SAS       A1                   F    80    35    3 11/21/86 12:16
   PROFILE  EXEC      A2                   V    23     8    1  9/30/86 12:22
```

```
   PF: 1 Hlp 2 Brw 3 End 4 Xed 5 Spl 6 /Sb 7 Scb 8 Scf 9 /Sd 10 /St 11 >I 12 Can
```

Place cursor at file _____ (your file name) LISTING A1 and
press F2. You will see your results on the next page. However,
you will note that they all do not fit on one screen.

Emphasize: the three different terms modifying your file name
are the following. The term LISTING refers to output, SAS
refers to analysis, and SASLOG refers to a running record by
which errors can be identified.

DESCRIPTIVE STATISTICS

VARIABLE	SUM	MEAN	UNCORRECTED SS
WA_FEATR	327.0000000	8.175000000	3539.000000
F	68.0000000	1.700000000	150.000000
INTERCEP	40.0000000	1.000000000	40.000000

VARIABLE	VARIANCE	STD DEVIATION
WA_FEATR	22.19935897	4.711619570
F	0.88205128	0.939175853
INTERCEP	0.00000000	0.000000000

DEP VARIABLE: WA_FEATR

ANALYSIS OF VARIANCE

SUM OF   MEAN

The file needs to be moved down so that you see the actual
number for the "standardized estimate" of the regression
coefficient in the output. To do this, type "Down 30" meaning
move screen down 30 lines. Press "enter." On p. 43 you will
see the actual standardized coefficient "0.47573096."

          C.V.   51.35747

                        PARAMETER ESTIMATES

                  PARAMETER   STANDARD   T FOR H0:
VARIABLE   DF   ESTIMATE   ERROR   PARAMETER=0   PROB > |T|

INTERCEP   1   4.11773256   1.38620619   2.971   0.0051
F   1   2.38662791   0.71583380   3.334   0.0019

                 STANDARDIZED
VARIABLE   DF   ESTIMATE

INTERCEP   1   0
F   1   0.47573096
* * * END OF FILE * * *

Note the value of the standardized coefficient 0.47573. This
is Step 10 (from the steps listed on page 18. Also, note the T
value of the coefficient and the significance level of that T.

Press F3 to get back to the list of files.

VI.   Procedure to Complete the CDM

You have now accomplished the most essential step of all your computer work. You have calculated a relationship in the CDM. This relation is the effect of information (F) upon the "Feature" dimension of the consumers' attitudes from Questions 4 and 6. To simplify, only this one dimension was used. That relationship you will recall from p. 43, is .47573096. Also, to simplify, two digits are enough, and so it is .47.

From now on throughout the course you will simply be repeating what you have just completed. The details will be a little different but the principles will be exactly the same as you have done so nicely up to this point.

You will now proceed to calculate the additional relationships in the CDM model. You do this by simply repeating the instructions beginning on p. 27 to add the necessary data for each additional equation needed. However, there the equation which is for the WA_FEATR variable, is already specified for you, as shown on p. 37. To add new equations and variables to your CDM model, follow the steps shown on subsequent pages.

```
LVL 0 -- A 191   900 BLKS 3375 R/W   8 FILES  4% -- FILE    1 OF      8
HOLDNESS SASLOG   A1                  V   90    25     2  3/24/87 15:20
HOLDNESS LISTING  A1                  V   76    45     2  3/24/87 15:20
HOLDNESS SAS      A1 __               F   80    16     2  3/24/87 15:17
GENERAL  SAS      A1                  F   80    20     2 12/02/86  9:48
VEGAAGG1 SAS      A1                  F   80    45     4 11/29/86 14:44
MAVRICK  SAS      A1                  F   80    42     4 11/21/86 15:02
WAGON    SAS      A1                  F   80    35     3 11/21/86 12:16
PROFILE  EXEC     A2                  V   23     8     1  9/30/86 12:22
```

PF: 1 Hlp 2 Brw 3 End 4 Xed 5 Spl 6 /Sb 7 Scb 8 Scf 9 /Sd 10 /St 11 >I 12 Can

Now, let us assume that you wish to add another equation in the
SAS program file. To do this, press F4 with cursor at _____
(your file name) SAS A1.

```
=====  * * * Top of File * * *
       |...+....1....+....2....+....3....+....4....+....5....+....6....+....7..
=====  OPTIONS PS = 60 LS = 80;
=====
=====  CMS FI GREEN DISK RCA DAT D;
=====
=====  DATA;
=====  INFILE GREEN;
=====  INPUT P_VD 1 P_RCA 2 I_PAST 3 I_FUTR 4 C 5
=====  A_PRICE 6 A_FEATR 7 A_NAME 8 A_MOVIE 9 B_PRICE 10
=====  B_FEATR 11 B_STOP 12 B_RECRD 13 B_RPRICE 14
=====  W_PRICE 15 W_FEATR 16 W_NAME 17 W_MOVIE 18
=====  F_FRND 19 F_TV 20 F_TVAD 21 F_SVC 22 F_CHLD 23
=====  F_CR 24 F_MAGZN 25 I_RCA 26;
=====  WA_FEATR = A_FEATR * W_FEATR;
=====  WA_NAME = A_NAME * W_NAME;
=====  F = F_CR + F_CHLD + F_TVAD;
=====  PROC REG SIMPLE; MODEL WA_FEATR = F /STB;
=====  * * * End of File * * *

====>
```

To add another equation from the CDM to the SAS Program, you
should type an I on the middle equal sign of the line after
which the new blank line for the equation is to be inserted (as
you will see on p. 47) and press "enter."

```
===== * * * Top of File * * *
      !...+....1....+....2....+....3....+....4....+....5....+....6....+....7..
===== OPTIONS PS = 60 LS = 80;
=====
===== CMS FI GREEN DISK RCA DAT D;
=====
===== DATA;
===== INFILE GREEN;
===== INPUT P_VD 1 P_RCA 2 I_PAST 3 I_FUTR 4 C 5
===== A_PRICE 6 A_FEATR 7 A_NAME 8 A_MOVIE 9 B_PRICE 10
===== B_FEATR 11 B_STOP 12 B_RECRD 13 B_RPRICE 14
===== W_PRICE 15 W_FEATR 16 W_NAME 17 W_MOVIE 18
===== F_FRND 19 F_TV 20 F_TVAD 21 F_SVC 22 F_CHLD 23
===== F_CR 24 F_MAGZN 25 I_RCA 26;
===== WA_FEATR = A_FEATR * W_FEATR;
===== WA_NAME = A_NAME * W_NAME;
=I=== F = F_CR + F_CHLD + F_TVAD;
===== PROC REG SIMPLE; MODEL WA_FEATR = F /STB;
===== * * * End of File * * *

====>
                                              X E D I T  1 File
```

As you notice the I now appears and when you press "enter" you
will see the space created for the new equation on p. 48.

```
=====  * * * Top of File * * *
       !...+....1....+....2....+....3....+....4....+....5....+....6....+....7..
=====  OPTIONS PS = 60 LS = 80;
=====
=====  CMS FI GREEN DISK RCA DAT A;
=====
=====  DATA;
=====  INFILE GREEN;
=====  INPUT P_VD 1 P_RCA 2 I_PAST 3 I_FUTR 4 C 5
=====  A_PRICE 6 A_FEATR 7 A_NAME 8 A_MOVIE 9 B_PRICE 10
=====  B_FEATR 11 B_STOP 12 B_RECRD 13 B_RPRICE 14
=====  W_PRICE 15 W_FEATR 16 W_NAME 17 W_MOVIE 18
=====  F_FRND 19 F_TV 20 F_TVAD 21 F_SVC 22 F_CHLD 23
=====  F_CR 24 F_MAGZN 25 I_RCA 26;
=====  WA_FEATR = A_FEATR * W_FEATR;
=====  WA_NAME = A_NAME * W_NAME;
=====  F = F_CR + F_CHLD + F_TVAD;
=====
=====  PROC REG SIMPLE; MODEL WA_FEATR = F /STB;
=====  * * * End of File * * *
====>
                                                     X E D I T  1 File
```

Now having learned the effect of information upon one key
attitude dimension of the RCA Videodisk, WA_FEATR, suppose you
want to know the effect of information on the B variable of the
CDM?

Type in the following changes to the program. First, you
operationally define B and enter it as the B equation.

$$B = B\_PRICE + B\_STOP + B\_RECRD + B\_RPRICE;$$

Second, you must, of course, also change the regression command
- PROC REG SIMPLE - to do this new regression for you. To
accomplish this you will have to change it to read, B = F/STB.
After typing the equation for B and modifying the PROC REG
statement, press "enter" and you see the next screen.

```
===== * * * Top of File * * *
      !...+....1....+....2....+....3....+....4....+....5....+....6....+....7..
===== OPTIONS PS = 60 LS = 80;
=====
===== CMS FI GREEN DISK RCA DAT A;
=====
===== DATA;
===== INFILE GREEN;
===== INPUT P_VD 1 P_RCA 2 I_PAST 3 I_FUTR 4 C 5
===== A_PRICE 6 A_FEATR 7 A_NAME 8 A_MOVIE 9 B_PRICE 10
===== B_FEATR 11 B_STOP 12 B_RECRD 13 B_RPRICE 14
===== W_PRICE 15 W_FEATR 16 W_NAME 17 W_MOVIE 18
===== F_FRND 19 F_TV 20 F_TVAD 21 F_SVC 22 F_CHLD 23
===== F_CR 24 F_MAGZN 25 I_RCA 26;
===== WA_FEATR = A_FEATR * W_FEATR;
===== WA_NAME = A_NAME * W_NAME;
===== F = F_CR + F_CHLD + F_TVAD;
===== B = B_PRICE + B_STOP + B_RECRD + B_RPRICE;
===== PROC REG SIMPLE; MODEL B = F /STB;
===== * * * End of File * * *
====>
```

X E D I T 1 File

Type "file" on command line (===>) to store the additions that
have been made to the SAS program.

```
===== * * * Top of File * * *
      !...+....1....+....2....+....3....+....4....+....5....+....6....+....7..
===== OPTIONS PS = 60 LS = 80;
=====
===== CMS FI GREEN DISK RCA DAT D;
=====
===== DATA;
===== INFILE GREEN;
===== INPUT P_VD 1 P_RCA 2 I_PAST 3 I_FUTR 4 C 5
===== A_PRICE 6 A_FEATR 7 A_NAME 8 A_MOVIE 9 B_PRICE 10
===== B_FEATR 11 B_STOP 12 B_RECRD 13 B_RPRICE 14
===== W_PRICE 15 W_FEATR 16 W_NAME 17 W_MOVIE 18
===== F_FRND 19 F_TV 20 F_TVAD 21 F_SVC 22 F_CHLD 23
===== F_CR 24 F_MAGZN 25 I_RCA 26;
===== WA_FEATR = A_FEATR * W_FEATR;
===== WA_NAME = A_NAME * W_NAME;
===== F = F_CR + F_CHLD + F_TVAD;
===== B = B_PRICE + B_STOP + B_RECRD + B_RPRICE;
===== PROC REG SIMPLE; MODEL B = F /STB;
===== * * * End of File * * *
====> file
```

X E D I T 1 File

As you notice here "file" now has been typed on the command
line. Press "enter" key to store file and return to the list
of files.

```
LVL 0 —— A 191      900 BLKS 3375 R/W        8 FILES  4% —— FILE        1 OF        8
HOLDNESS SASLOG    A1                          V    90     25      2  3/24/87 15:20
HOLDNESS LISTING   A1                          V    76     45      2  3/24/87 15:20
HOLDNESS SAS       A1 *EDIT                     F    80     17      2  3/24/87 16:06
GENERAL  SAS       A1                           F    80     20      2 12/02/86  9:48
VEGAAGG1 SAS       A1                           F    80     45      4 11/29/86 14:44
MAVRICK  SAS       A1                           F    80     42      4 11/21/86 15:02
WAGON    SAS       A1                           F    80     35      3 11/21/86 12:16
PROFILE  EXEC      A2                           V    23      8      1  9/30/86 12:22



       PF: 1 Hlp 2 Brw 3 End 4 Xed 5 Spl 6 /Sb 7 Scb 8 Scf 9 /Sd 10 /St 11 >I 12 Can
```

Now to get out of the list of files to the CMS ready prompt to
run the regression on the new equation, press F3.

sas holdness

Type "SAS ____ (your file)" and press the "enter" key. This
causes the regression to run as indicated on p. 53 where you
will see that it is completed, "Job Completed" or by repeating
the CMS ready prompt, i.e., "R;   T=0.(time)."

SAS VERSION 5.08 COLUMBIA BUSINESS SCHOOL

Running HOLDNESS SAS

Job Completed.
R; T=1.01/2.23 16:07:17

RUNNING   CUGSBVM

Press F10 to get back to the file list and Press F9 to get the
most recently created file first in the list.

```
LVL 0 --- A 191     900 BLKS 3375 R/W     16 FILES 12% -- FILE      1 OF      16
HOLDNESS LISTING   A1 __              V    81    45    2  2/05/85 12:32
HOLDNESS SASLOG    A1                 V   133    40    2  2/05/85 12:32
HOLDNESS SAS       A1                 F    80    17    2  2/05/85 12:31
FAST1    SAS       A1                 F    80    83    7  2/05/85 12:24
SIMM     SAS       A1                 F    80    61    5  2/05/85 12:24
SIMV     SAS       A1                 F    80    67    6  2/05/85 12:23
SIMW     SAS       A1                 F    80    64    5  2/05/85 12:22
JPL8     SAS       A1                 F    80    84    7  2/05/85 12:21
JPL7     SAS       A1                 F    80    82    7  2/05/85 12:20
JPL6     SAS       A1                 F    80    82    7  2/05/85 12:20
GENINPT  SAS       A1                 F    80    20    2  2/05/85 12:18
VINPT    SAS       A1                 F    80    29    3  2/05/85 12:18
WINPT    SAS       A1                 F    80    29    3  2/05/85 12:18
MINPT    SAS       A1                 F    80    28    3  2/05/85 12:18
PROFILE  EXEC      A1                 V    23     6    1  2/24/87 15:41
B860101A NETLOG    A0                 V   106    11    2  1/05/85 12:32


PF: 1 Hlp 2 Brw 3 End 4 Xed 5 Spl 6 /Sb 7 Scb 8 Scf 9 /Sd 10 /St 11 >I 12 Can
```

Press F2 with cursor on (your file) _____ LISTING to "browse"
the results of the regression, as indicated by "2 Brw" at bottom
of list of files on this page.

DESCRIPTIVE STATISTICS

VARIABLE	SUM	MEAN	UNCORRECTED SS
B	91.00000000	2.275000000	259.0000000
F	68.00000000	1.700000000	150.0000000
INTERCEP	40.00000000	1.000000000	40.0000000

VARIABLE	VARIANCE	STD DEVIATION
B	1.332692308	1.154422933
F	0.882051282	0.939175853
INTERCEP	0.000000000	0.000000000

1
                                      SAS   13:10 FRIDAY, FEBRUARY 5, 1985

DEP VARIABLE: B

ANALYSIS OF VARIANCE

SUM OF   MEAN

Note however, on the screen above to the far right, that
"standardized estimate" does not appear. Hence, as before, on
p. 42 type "Down 30" on command line (===>) and press "enter"
to move down the screen to make room for the coefficient.

If it is necessary to move screen to the right to show "standardized estimate," while in F2 Browse screen, type "Right 20"
and press "enter."

                   C.V.   38.19594

                            PARAMETER ESTIMATES

                    PARAMETER   STANDARD   T FOR HO:
VARIABLE   DF   ESTIMATE   ERROR   PARAMETER=0   PROB > !T!

INTERCEP   1   0.87645349   0.28690292   3.055   0.0041
F   1   0.82267442   0.14815603   5.553   0.0001

                  STANDARDIZED
VARIABLE   DF   ESTIMATE

INTERCEP   1   0
F   1   0.66928326
* * * END OF FILE * * *

Having seen your results - a regression coefficient of .669283
- you want to exit the browse mode by pressing F3 which puts
you back into the list of files. You may wish to have a hard
copy of the output shown above, and if so, you can press
shift-PrtSc at your file LISTING while Browsing this file.

You may also get a printed copy of the entire LISTING file
(rather than just a screenful) printed on the mainframe printer. Return to the list of files from BROWSE (press F3) and
type PRINT next to the file you want to print. Press "enter."

```
LVL 0 —— A 191    900 BLKS 3375 R/W    8 FILES  4% —— FILE    1 OF    8
HOLDNESS LISTING  A1 __              V   76    45    2  3/24/87 16:07
HOLDNESS SASLOG   A1                 V   90    26    2  3/24/87 16:07
HOLDNESS SAS      A1                 F   80    17    2  3/24/87 16:06
GENERAL  SAS      A1                .F   80    20    2 12/02/86  9:48
VEGAAGGI SAS      A1                 F   80    45    4 11/29/86 14:44
MAVRICK  SAS      A1                 F   80    42    4 11/21/86 15:02
WAGON    SAS      A1                 F   80    35    3 11/21/86 12:16
PROFILE  EXEC     A2                 V   23     8    1  9/30/86 12:22
```

PF: 1 Hlp 2 Brw 3 End 4 Xed 5 Spl 6 /Sb 7 Scb 8 Scf 9 /Sd 10 /St 11 >I 12 Can

You can now do the remaining equations as listed below by
simply proceeding, as you did on p. 46 and following, to insert
new equations and to run them.

Or you may prefer to get out of the list of files and into the
CMS ready prompt where you can log off. To do these last two
steps of getting back to the CMS ready prompt and logging off,
press F3 while in the list of files and then type "LOGOFF," and
press "enter."

VII. Conclusion

You have now modeled two relations of the CDM, F to a simplified A variable and F to the B variable. Now to complete the CDM, you simply repeat Sec. VI by inserting the remaining equations, one at a time:

$$F \rightarrow C$$
$$B \rightarrow A$$
$$B \rightarrow C$$
$$A \rightarrow I$$
$$C \rightarrow I$$
$$I \rightarrow D$$

You can now move on to the more complex cases:

Lean Strips

Chevrolet Vega Case

Central Assets Accounts (Merrill/Lynch, Shearson, Dean

Witter, and Citicorp).

Quick'n Easy II will prepare you to model any of the above three cases. However, you may find it easier once you have set up the new case with Quick'n Easy II, to come back to p. 46 to Quick'n Easy I to actually carry out much of the modeling, at least on the first line of the remaining cases, Lean Strips.

The following pages illustrate the final step (of the 12 steps on page 18) in using the IBM 4341, logging off.

R; T=0.08/0.20 21:35:34

You can see the process of logging off has begun. If you will
press the "enter" key, you will see on p. 60 that logging off
has been accomplished and the time that it was completed. This
logging off is essential because, if you do not, it will be
impossible to log back on the same account from a different PC.

You have now worked completely through steps 1 through 11 on
p. 18. Then, when you added the equation on p. 45, you again
worked through steps 3 through 11, but this time you logged
off, which took you through step 12.

This is a major accomplishment, and from here on, you will
largely be repeating what you have done here.

```
R; T=0.08/0.20 21:35:34
log
CONNECT= 00:57:44 VIRTCPU= 000:03.08 TOTCPU= 000:08.29
LOGOFF AT 21:37:57 EST TUESDAY 11/12/85
```

II Summary

Now, having logged off, you should go back to p. 18 and
review the typical sequence of events. Try to recall the
various events in going through the RCA Case and identify them
in the list so that you acquire a real sense of this list of
events. To do so will help you immensely in doing the next
three cases: Lean Strips, Vega, and Cash/Asset Accounts.

A review of the ten activities performed between logging
on and logging off as listed on p. 18 can be very helpful in
fixing them in your mind for future use. First, in Step 2 you
needed the beginning of a SAS program (p. 35) to which you
would add whatever procedures are needed to carry out your
analysis. It was obtained by copying it from the RCAINPT SAS D

file as you did on p. 35 and naming it with your own unique file name.

The third step (p. 36) was to enter the list of files available to you from which you could choose the specific program you wish to work with. Step 4 (p. 37) was to enter that selected SAS program using the Executive Editor which enabled you to modify the program to get it to do what you wanted it to do (in directing the VM).

Now having access to the Executive Editor to build the program you would ordinarily proceed to insert your commands as to what it should do, e.g., run a regression of certain variables.

In future practice, in Step 5 you will modify the program by inserting the procedures you wish to have carried out, e.g., a particular regression, correlation, frequency table, etc., in giving you the answers to the questions you have, as seen in pages 45-48, where the variable B was defined and the regression equation changed to use B instead of WA_FEATR.

In Step 6 you saved the changes so that they will be carried out and also so that you get out of the Executive Editor (p. 50).

In Step 7 you get out of the list of files so as to run the designated procedure (p. 51) and in Step 8 you told it to actually run the procedure (p. 52). In Step 9 you entered the list of files as a means of browsing the output of the procedure (p. 54). In Step 10 you actually saw the output (pages 55-56). In Step 11 you probably made a printed copy of the output as you often will in the future. In your analyses of the other cases you will proceed repeatedly through steps 3-11 until you have completed the analysis of the case that you have chosen to do at the moment.

```
OPTIONS PS = 60 LS = 132;

CMS FI GREEN DISK RCA DAT D;

DATA;
INFILE GREEN;
INPUT P_VD 1 P_RCA 2 I_PAST 3 I_FUTR 4 C 5
A_PRICE 6 A_FEATR 7 A_NAME 8 A_MOVIE 9 B_PRICE 10
B_FEATR 11 B_STOP 12 B_RECRD 13 B_RPRICE 14
W_PRICE 15 W_FEATR 16 W_NAME 17 W_MOVIE 18
F_FRND 19 F_TV 20 F_TVAD 21 F_SVC 22 F_CHLD 23
F_CR 24 F_MAGZN 25 I_RCA 26;

WA_FEATR = A_FEATR * W_FEATR;
WA_NAME = A_NAME * W_NAME;
WA_MOVIE = A_MOVIE * W_MOVIE;
WA = WA_FEATR + WA_NAME + WA_MOVIE;
B = B_PRICE + B_STOP + B_RECRD + B_RPRICE;
F = F_CR + F_CHLD + F_TVAD;

PROC REG SIMPLE;
  MODEL C = F /STB;
PROC REG SIMPLE;
  MODEL WA = F /STB;
PROC REG SIMPLE;
  MODEL B = F /STB;
PROC REG SIMPLE;
  MODEL WA = B /STB;
PROC REG SIMPLE;
  MODEL C = B /STB;
PROC REG SIMPLE;
  MODEL I_RCA = C;
PROC REG SIMPLE;
  MODEL I_RCA = WA /STB;
PROC REG SIMPLE;
  MODEL P_RCA = I_RCA /STB;
```

Chapter 3

"Quick 'n Easy" II Computer Applications

for

Consumer Behavior in Marketing Strategy

1. INTRODUCTION

The purpose here is to provide you with some additional commands and procedures that were not included in Quick 'N Easy I, but which can be very useful in doing the three additional cases. It is assumed here that you are somewhat familiar with Quick 'N Easy I (QE I). There will be some overlap with QE I, e.g., you may wish to do additional analysis on the RCA case that you used in QE I.

*Prepared by John Stephan and John A. Howard. We wish to thank Sally Strickholm and Robert Coletti for their splendid early work in preparing this document.

This is an introductory manual to SAS programming. Although the software package is not interactive, it is quite easy to master the modest amount of SAS programming needed to develop the Customer Decision Model (CDM). As with any introductory document, only the very basics are discussed. There is a vast amount of SAS programming available and many more sophisticated procedures which can be performed. However, this manual does provide all the information that is required to complete assignments.

For the beginner, the prospect of working with a mainframe computer in a programming language can be intimidating. However, let me assure you that the IBM 4341 computer with its VM/CMS operating system is quite manageable. What is needed is an understanding of the work flow of a typical computer session which I have provided below. If you comprehend and remember it, your computer sessions will be much more organized, efficient, and pleasant.

This is a typical sequence of events in a computer session for modeling consumer behavior:

1) Log onto the computer.

2) Copy the SAS program you need to use from the D disk to the A disk with the COPY command.

3) Enter the list of files (SAS programs and other files).

4) Enter a desired SAS program using the Executive Editor.

5) Modify the program.

6) Save changes and exit the program.

7 Exit the list of files.

8) Run the modified SAS program.

9) Enter the list of files again.

10) Look at the SAS output file.

11) Print the output file.

12) Log off. (You may repeat steps 3 - 11 many times before logging off. However, do not forget to log off.)

This list obviously provides information on "what to do's" and not "how to do's." However, after .reading the remainder of this manual you will learn how to do each of the above steps. If, during a computer session, you remember what you should be doing, it is easy for you to look it up. Refer to these 11 basic steps when first working with the computer until you have become familiar with the routine. It will save you a great deal of agony. Good luck and have fun with the course!

LOGGING ONTO THE IBM 4341

The log on procedure is very straightforward. It is slightly different depending on whether you are working in the business school computer lab or from a remote location.

WORKING AT THE BUSINESS SCHOOL: You need to check out a Y-term diskette from the computer attendant. Place the disk in the A drive of your P.C. and either turn the machine on or re-boot the PC if it is already turned on. (To re-boot, hit the DEL key while holding down the CTRL and ALT keys.)

Note: YOU NEED TO USE A P.C. THAT HAS A RED DOT ON THE SIDE OF THE TERMINAL. BLUE DOT TERMINALS DO NOT CONNECT TO THE MAINFRAME.

FROM A REMOTE LOCATION: All instructions above for logging on from the business school apply (with the exception of the need for a red dot terminal). However, you will need to use a modem to connect to the computer through telephone lines. Instructions for using the modem will be provided.

Subsequent pages provide the computer screens that you will encounter during log on procedure. The Y-term program is an interactive program for the most part. Supplemental instructions are provided below each screen where needed. Turn the page to see the first screen.

```
================================================================================
||                      Columbia Business School                             ||
||                    James L. Dohr Computer Center                          ||
||                  Yterm Version 1.2 April 8, 1985                          ||
================================================================================
Current date is Tue 1-01-1980
Enter New Date:
Current Time is 00:00:01
Enter New Time:
```

====> PRESS THE ENTER KEY TWICE

```
Starting Yterm Program....
=======================================================================
||       If dialing in, tell Yale ASCII the terminal type is IBMPC  ||
||                 To switch color on hit keypad 5 d                ||
||                 To make tab key work hit keypad 5 c              ||
||            Hit Ctrl-Break to exit to DOS after logging off.      ||
=======================================================================
Strike a key when ready...
```

```
====> PRESS ANY KEY
====>
====> If you are dialing in, dial the phone number (212-280-8763),
====> or issue the command to instruct the modem to dial
====> (e.g., ATDT2808763).  PRESS the ENTER key.

====> In BOTH cases, next, hold the Ctrl key down and press the NUM
====> LOCK key once.  Then press the ENTER key.  This signals the
====> computer to recognize your request to be connected.  You should
====> see that beginning of the screen shown on the next page.
```

```
COLUMBIA BUSINESS SCHOOL - DOHR COMPUTER CENTER
Services Available : IBM4341 or IBM3705
SERVICE?  ibm4341

WELCOME TO CUGSBVM !
CONNECTED

ENTER TERMINAL TYPE:
VALID TYPES ARE:
ADM31      ADM3A      IBM3101    DM1520     DM1521
DM3045     VT100      TVI912     TVI920     TVI950
TVI950R    HARDCOPY   TYPETERM   PLOTTER
IBMPC      IBM3101A   ADM3ALT    DM1520A
VT52A      DECPRO     C108A      Z19A       H19A       HP2621A    HP2648A
RLG40A     CUCCA-PC   CUCCA-DM
ENTER TERMINAL TYPE: ibmpc
```

```
====> ENTER IBM4341 and press the ENTER key at the prompt for SERVICE?
====> ENTER IBMPC and press ENTER key at the prompt for TERMINAL TYPE:
```

You will then see the screen on the next page.......

```
    GGGGGGG
GGG     GGG
GG       GG   $$$$$$
GG            $$      $$$
GG   GGGG     $$              BBBBBB
GG   GGGG     $$              BBB  BBB
GG     GG    $$$$$            BB    BB
GGG    GGG         $$         BBB  BBB
  GGGGGGG          $$         BBBBBB              VM/SP
            $$$    $$         BBB  BB             4.0
              $$$$$$$         BB     BB
                              BB     BB
                              BBB  BBB
                              BBBBBB
```

Columbia Business School
James L. Dohr Computer Center
Network Node: CUGSBVM

                                              RUNNING   CUGSBVM
(c) Copyright 1983, 1984 Yale University, All Rights Reserved.

====> PRESS THE ENTER KEY

You will then see the screen on the next page.....

Enter one of the following commands:

```
LOGON userid           (Example:  LOGON VMUSER1)
DIAL userid            (Example:  DIAL VMUSER2)
MSG userid message     (Example:  MSG VMUSER2 GOOD MORNING)
LOGOFF
```

```
====> ENTER L and your ACCOUNT NUMBER  (e.g, B860101A-H), and press
====> ENTER
```

```
Enter one of the following commands:

LOGON userid              (Example:  LOGON VMUSER1)
DIAL userid               (Example:  DIAL VMUSER2)
MSG userid message        (Example:  MSG VMUSER2 GOOD MORNING)
LOGOFF

L B860101A
ENTER PASSWORD  (IT WILL NOT APPEAR WHEN TYPED):
```

```
====> ENTER the PASSWORD for the ACCOUNT, and press the ENTER key
```

Enter one of the following commands:

```
LOGON userid          (Example:  LOGON VMUSER1)
DIAL userid           (Example:  DIAL VMUSER2)
MSG userid message    (Example:  MSG VMUSER2 GOOD MORNING)
LOGOFF

L B860101A
ENTER PASSWORD  (IT WILL NOT APPEAR WHEN TYPED):

DASD 190 LINKED R/O; R/W BY MAINT; R/O BY 051 USERS
DASD 19E LINKED R/O; R/W BY MAINT; R/O BY 048 USERS
LOGMSG - 10:45:49 EST SATURDAY 10/26/85
* TDISK ARE NOT PERMANENT STORAGE.  THEY MAY DISAPPEAR AT ANY TIME.
*
* SYNCSORT NOW ONLINE ... SEE HELP FOR MORE DETAILS.
*
* UPLOAD AND DOWNLOAD EXECS NOW ALLOW FOR MULTIPLE FILE PC TRANSFERS.
LOGON AT 20:40:12 EST TUESDAY 11/12/85
VM/SP REL 2 04/25/84 10:50
```

```
====> PRESS the ENTER key.  (If "MORE..." appears, press "+" key)
```

```
Enter one of the following commands:

LOGON userid            (Example:  LOGON VMUSER1)
DIAL userid             (Example:  DIAL VMUSER2)
MSG userid message      (Example:  MSG VMUSER2 GOOD MORNING)
LOGOFF


L B860101A
ENTER PASSWORD  (IT WILL NOT APPEAR WHEN TYPED):

DASD 190 LINKED R/O; R/W BY MAINT; R/O BY 051 USERS
DASD 19E LINKED R/O; R/W BY MAINT; R/O BY 048 USERS
LOGMSG - 10:45:49 EST SATURDAY 10/26/85
* TDISK ARE NOT PERMANENT STORAGE.  THEY MAY DISAPPEAR AT ANY TIME.
*
* SYNCSORT NOW ONLINE ... SEE HELP FOR MORE DETAILS.
*
* UPLOAD AND DOWNLOAD EXECS NOW ALLOW FOR MULTIPLE FILE PC TRANSFERS.
LOGON AT 20:40:12 EST TUESDAY 11/12/85
VM/SP REL 2 04/25/84 10:50


'19E' REPLACES ' Y (19E) '
Y(19E) R/O
SHARED YSTAT NOT AVAILABLE.
D (192) R/O
R; T=0.11/0.31  19:30:20
```

```
====> YOU ARE NOW LOGGED IN
```

Before you begin, a few concepts are essential to deal effectively with the IBM 4341. Recall from Quick 'N Easy I that once you successfully issued the logon command you saw VM READ in the lower right hand corner of the screen. At this time you were in communication with the VM operating system which controls the computer's physical devices (tape and disk drives, the central processing unit, system printer, etc.). You were instructed to hit the "enter" key to get into the CMS environment. (Recall that the ready prompt in CMS is:

R; T=0.01/0.01.

You should then see the word RUNNING in the lower right hand corner of the screen.) The CMS operating system, which reads various programming languages, (such as SAS) allows the user to communicate with VM and, therefore, permits the user to access the real physical devices. (The user writes a program which CMS reads and communicates to VM which in turn tells the actual computer what to do.)

To instruct the computer to perform functions for you, CMS commands are entered to the system. In addition, several of the function keys to the left of the keyboard, have special meanings associated with them for instructing the system to perform certain, frequently performed tasks. All CMS commands are issued when the screen is displaying VM READ in the lower right hand corner of the screen. The command is typed in the lower left corner of the screen, along with any parameters, or extra information, that may be required, and the ENTER key is pressed. If the command was issued correctly, it will be performed.

If you made an error, however, such as mistyping the command word, or supplying incorrect parameters, the system will respond with a ready prompt that includes a CMS RETURN CODE:

R(#####); T=0.01/0.01.]

¦ return code

This return code itself will not provide any information, except the fact that an error has occurred. Occasionally an error message containing a brief description of the error will accompany the return code. If a message was not printed, you must carefully look at the command you typed to discern what was incorrectly entered, and retype the entire command to issue it again.

3.1 CMS Commands

Below are a list of CMS commands which are to be executed at the CMS ready prompt, "R; T=0.01/0.01."

SAS   This is the run command. You issue this command in conjunction with a particular SAS program. By typing:

                SAS LEARN1

                you will cause the computer to run the program, LEARN1 SAS.

COPY   Copies a particular file. This command is used if a second copy of a file is desired.

                At least one part of the filename must be changed with the COPY command (either FILENAME, FILETYPE, or FILEMODE. See section 5, page 89, for a discussion of file naming convention: filename, filetype, and filemode). The second (new) file must not already exist.

                You will need the COPY command to obtain a copy of the SAS program that applies to the data you plan to analyze with SAS (see Section 11 for a list of datafiles and programs). Remember that one of the first steps in QE I was to copy RCAINPT SAS A to a file with a name you chose.

                To issue the COPY command, you must type :

                COPY OLDFN OLDFT OLDFM NEWFN NEWFT NEWFM

                Where:

                - OLDFN = OLD FILENAME   (e.g., RCAINPT);

                - OLDFT = OLD FILETYPE   (e.g., SAS);

                - OLDFM = OLD FILEMODE   (e.g., D);

                - NEWFN = NEW FILENAME   (e.g., RCAINPT - same as old filename);

                - NEWFT = NEW FILETYPE   (e.g., SAS - same as old filetype);

- NEWFM = NEW FILEMODE   (e.g., A - different from old filemode).

So if, for example, you were planning to analyze the LEANSTRIPS data, you would need to obtain a copy of the SAS program LEANINPT SAS D. The following command would accomplish this:

COPY LEANINPT SAS D _____ SAS A (REPLACE)

The blank in the above command is filled in with a name of your choosing. The (REPLACE) parameter is necessary to insure that if the second (new) file already exists, it will be overwritten with a new copy of LEANINPT SAS.

If you wish, this COPY command can be performed by returning to the familiar Quick 'N Easy I, p. 35. You can proceed there to analyze the LEANSTRIPS data as described here, but in a more guided and familiar framework.

RENAME
Renames a particular file. Execute exactly as you would the COPY command. You must type :

RENAME OLDFN OLDFT OLDFM NEWFN NEWFT NEWFM

ERASE
Erases a file from storage. To erase the file LEARN1 SASLOG A, you would type:

ERASE LEARN1 SASLOG A

FLIST
This command stands for file list and will display the list of files on your A (default) disk. You may alternatively press the F10 function key to perform the FLIST command. (See Section 6, DISK AVAILABILITY, for a discussion of the various disks at your disposal.)

HX
Halt eXecution: Allows you to stop a SAS program that is running.

BEGIN
Allows you to get back to VM and CMS if you've been thrown out to CP READ. (Look in lower right hand corner to find CP READ.)

I CMS
Allows you to get back to VM and CMS if you've been thrown out to CP READ. (Look in lower right hand corner). BEGIN is preferable to I CMS to get back to CMS, but BEGIN does not work under all circumstances.

LOG
This is the logoff command. You must remember to issue this command at the end of each session, otherwise it

83

will be impossible to log back on to the same account from a different terminal.

4.   The FLIST Screen

The FLIST command, described above, brings a list of all files on
your A disk onto the screen. Many different functions are available
from this screen.   We will briefly describe the sections of this
screen, so that you will understand the information presented. Following this, the various commands available from the FLIST screen will be
presented.

SAMPLE FLIST SCREEN

COLUMNS:
==

A Name	B Type	C Mode	D Commands	E Format	F Length	G #Recs	H #Blks	I Date	J Time

==

HOLDNESS	LISTING	A1		V	81	27	2	12/12/85	20:04
HOLDNESS	SASLOG	A1		V	133	36	2	12/12/85	20:04
HOLDNESS	SAS	A1		F	80	17	2	12/12/85	19:55
ORIGINAL	SAS	A1		F	80	44	3	12/05/85	11:12
PROFILE	EXEC	A1		V	23	7	1	7/17/85	12:17

1=HLP 2=BRW 3=END 4=XED 5=SPL 6=/SB 7=SCB 8=SCF 9=/SD 10=/ST 11=>I
12=CA

The sample FLIST screen above will serve to illustrate examples of the
commands that can be issued from the FLIST screen.   Two additional

85

lines have been added at the top of this screen to help us in describing the various columns of information presented. These lines will NOT appear when you give the FLIST command on the system.

COLUMN	DESCRIPTION
A	FILENAME. This column contains the file name for each file stored on the A Disk.
B	FILETYPE. This column contains the file type for each file stored on the A Disk.
C	FILEMODE. Always A followed by a number. The number is unimportant.

Columns A, B, and C for each line on the screen, comprise the full file name specification for each file. |
D	This is the command area into which various commands, discussed later, are entered.
E	Record format. F=fixed, which means all lines in the file have the same number of characters. V=variable which means that each line of a file may have a different number of characters from any other. SAS programs must have a format of F.
F	Record length. For FIXED files, the record length indicates how many characters each line in the file has. For VARIABLE files, the record length indicates the length of the longest record in the file. All SAS programs have record lengths of 80.
G	Number of records. This number tells how many lines (records) are in the file.
H	Number of blocks. Your A disk is divided into 900 blocks of 1024 bytes each of disk storage. This column tells how many of these blocks each file occupies.
I and J	These two columns are the date and time, respectively, that the file was last changed.

4.1 FLIST Function Keys

At the bottom of the screen is a line telling you what all of the function keys do while the FLIST screen is displayed. There are seven function keys of importance:

F1(=HLP)	HELP. Puts you into HELP mode. You may select any item from the HELP screen by moving the cursor to the item

and pressing F1 again. F3 pressed successively backs you out of HELP and returns you to the FLIST screen.

F2(=BRW)   BROWSE. Allows you to look at the file alongside the cursor without changing it.

F3(=END)   QUIT. Gets you out of FLIST and back to CMS.

F4(=XED)   XEDIT. Puts you into XEDIT, the executive editor, with the file along side the cursor when F4 was pressed.

F7(=SCB)   Screen Back. Moves the list of files one screen backward (toward the top of the list).

F8(=SCF)   Screen Forward. Moves the list of files one screen forward to display files lower down in the list that cannot all fit on one screen.

F9(=/SD)   Sort by date. Will sort the list of files so that those created or modified most recently will appear at the top of the list.

The cursor has been positioned next to the HOLDNESS SAS A1 file. Commands are typed in the area where the cursor is positioned (after the FILEMODE column).

4.2 FLIST Commands

Below is a list of commands which can be used once you have entered the list or directory of files. These commands affect the file alongside the cursor. When you have typed the command and any accompanying information needed, press the ENTER key to execute the command.

COPY   Will copy file alongside cursor to a second file. For example, to copy the file HOLDNESS SAS A to NEWHOLD SAS A, position the cursor next to the HOLDNESS SAS A file on the FLIST screen and type:

              COPY / NEWHOLD SAS A

              Then press ENTER. The slash (/) takes the place of the whole filename, HOLDNESS SAS A, so that you don't have to type that much.

ERASE	This command will erase the file which the blinking cursor is alongside of.
PRINT	This command will print the file which the blinking cursor is alongside of. This printout is done on the main system printer for the 4341 computer. An example of PRINTing is shown on the following FLIST screen.
RENAME	Will rename file alongside cursor to a second file. For example, to rename the file HOLDNESS SAS A to NEWHOLD SAS A, position the cursor next to the HOLDNESS SAS A file on the FLIST screen and type:

REN / NEWHOLD SAS A

Then press ENTER. The slash (/) takes the place of the whole filename, HOLDNESS SAS A, so that you don't have to type that much. RENAME can be abbreviated to REN.

SAMPLE PRINT COMMAND from FLIST SCREEN

COLUMNS:

```
===============================================================
   A         B        C       D        E       F       G      H      I       J
 Name      Type     Mode  Commands Format Length  #Recs  #Blks Date    Time
===============================================================

HOLDNESS LISTING   A1 PRINT  __        V      81      27      2 12/12/85 20:04
HOLDNESS SASLOG    A1                   V     133      36      2 12/12/85 20:04
HOLDNESS SAS       A1                   F      80      17      2 12/12/85 19:55
ORIGINAL SAS       A1                   F      80      44      3 12/05/85 11:12
PROFILE  EXEC      A1                   V      23       7      1  7/17/85 12:17
```

1=HLP 2=BRW 3=END 4=XED 5=SPL 6=/SB 7=SCB 8=SCF 9=/SD 10=/ST 11=>I
12=CA

PRESS ENTER to print the file HOLDNESS LISTING A1 on the mainframe printer.

5. FILE NAMING CONVENTION

There is a particular format for naming a file on the mainframe computer. As you will notice once you enter the directory of files on your account, there are three parts to a file name: FILENAME (also called FILEID), FILETYPE, and FILEMODE (in that order). FILENAME is the unique word which identifies each program in a directory. FILETYPE is the word which identifies which kind the file is. FILEMODE tells on which disk the file is located. For example, the file named LEARN1 SAS A would be a SAS program (filetype) called LEARN1 (filename) located on the A disk (filemode). Both words, FILENAME and FILETYPE can be up to eight alphanumeric characters in length. The file mode is a single letter, although you will notice the number 1 following each FILEMODE letter in your directory. It is not necessary to specify this number when referring to a particular file.

Besides the SAS filetype file, there will be several other kinds that you will encounter. In particular, you will run across two other SAS filetypes: SASLOG and LISTING. The SASLOG is produced every time you run a SAS program. It is an account of the computer's run of the program and will highlight any errors that may be in the program.

The SASLOG will have the same filename as the SAS program from which it was created. For example, if the program LEARN1 SAS is run, the computer will produce the file, LEARN1 SASLOG.

If there are no errors in the program, the computer will produce a second file called LEARN1 LISTING. This is the file which contains the statistical output from the program LEARN1 SAS.

6.   DISK AVAILABILITY

There are several disks available for each of the student accounts in the class. We are concerned only with two of these disks: A and D. The A disk is a Read/Write disk and is also referred to as the default disk. (It is called the default disk because if no filemode is mentioned it will default to the A disk.) This is the primary disk that each of you will be working with. Each student account has its own unique A disk.

The D disk is a Read Only disk. Each student account shares the same D disk. This D disk is also the A disk on the Teacher Master Account. It is on the Master Account's A disk (your D disk) that the instructor has stored the data for each of your assignments. Whenever you are trying to use the case data, you must be sure to use the D FILEMODE in the file definition statements of your programs. (See section 9.2, page 102, The RCA Example, for an illustration of the use of the D FILEMODE.)

7. <u>EXECUTIVE EDITOR (XEDIT)</u>]

There are two ways of entering a file using XEDIT for editing purposes:

1. From the CMS prompt, "R; T=0.01/0.01", type:

        X FILENAME FILETYPE FILEMODE.

Once you have done this for a particular file, the program will appear on the screen in the XEDIT mode (notice the word XEDIT in the lower right corner of the screen). You may also create new programs from scratch in this fashion by typing X followed by a file naming convention (FILENAME, FILETYPE, and FILEMODE) which is not already in your directory of files.

2. The suggested method is to enter the directory of files by typing FLIST (or pressing the F10 key) at the CMS prompt. Move the cursor alongside the file you wish to edit, and strike the F4 key. This automatically puts you into the XEDIT mode. (Again, notice the word XEDIT in the lower right hand corner of the screen.)

XEDIT is a simple full-screen editor. It has two basic modes of operation:

Command Mode   Commands are always entered to XEDIT in one of two
                 places:

                 1. On the Command Line. This is the right-pointing
                     arrow (===>)at the bottom left of the XEDIT screen.
                     Once the command is entered, the ENTER key is
                     pressed. Commands allow you to SAVE text you have
                     entered, move the screen forward or backward to
                     look at different parts of your text, and exit from
                     XEDIT.

93

2. In the Prefix Area. The prefix area is the column of equal signs (======) on the left-hand side of the screen. Prefix commands allow you to delete and insert lines within your text. Once again, a prefix command is typed, and the ENTER key is pressed.

Input Mode   To enter text into XEDIT, you must open up some blank lines on the screen and then input the text onto these newly created blank lines. Any text that is entered into the main body of the XEDIT screen (that is, not on the Command Line or in the Prefix Area) is considered text and is accepted as part of the file you are editing.

7.1 Inserting and Deleting Characters

To edit or make changes to text that you have already entered, simply use the arrow keys on the right of the keyboard to move the cursor to the desired position and type in changes. Newly typed characters will overwrite those already existing. If you want to insert some extra characters between existing characters without overwriting any, press the INSERT key, marked Ins, before typing the new characters. To turn off insert mode, press the Ins key again. When insert mode is on a little star character appears in the lower left corner of the screen.

The DEL key and the delete arrow key are used to remove (delete) characters from the text. The DEL key removes the character immediately above the cursor. The delete arrow key (above the return key) deletes the character immediately to the left of the cursor.

The minus key on the far right of the keyboard may be used to delete all characters from the cursor's position to the end of that line.

There are countless features in XEDIT to facilitate editing of a file. We will go through those features which we feel are most relevant for your work.

7.2   Inserting New Blank Lines

As mentioned previously, to enter new lines into a file, it is necessary to first "open up" some new blank lines, and then type the desired inserts onto them. The following is a description of how to insert these new blank lines.

Using the directional keys on the right hand side of the keyboard, move the cursor into left dashed (prefix) area beside the line of the program after which you wish to insert new blank lines. Type the letter I and a number next to it representing the number of new lines you wish to insert. By subsequently striking the "enter" key, the new lines will appear beneath the line you are currently on. (Example: I3 will insert 3 new lines; see the following page.)

At this point, you may find it easier to use the familiar procedures presented in "Quick 'N Easy I". The process of adding to an existing SAS program is discussed there, beginning on page 45.

To add 3 blank lines to a file:

SAMPLE   FILE   A1   F   80   TRUNC=80 SIZE=5 LINE=0 COLUMN=1

====== * * * TOP OF FILE * * *
        |...+....1....+....2....+....3....+....4....+....5....+....6...
======   This is a sample text file. New lines will be inserted
====== after this paragraph with the insert command. I3 is typed on
====== the prefix area of the last line of this paragraph. Return is
====== then pressed.
======   When the return is pressed, three blank lines will appear
====== before this paragraph. The cursor is placed at the first new
====== line. Once the new blank lines are inserted, you may type text
====== onto them.
======   * * * END OF FILE * * *

===>
                                             X E D I T   1   FILE

After the ENTER key is pressed, the changed file looks like this:

SAMPLE   FILE   A1   F   80   TRUNC=80 SIZE=8 LINE=0 COLUMN=1

====== * * * TOP OF FILE * * *
        |...+....1....+....2....+....3....+....4....+....5....+....6...
======   This is a sample text file. New lines will be inserted after
====== prefix this paragraph with the insert command. I3 is typed on
====== the area of the last line of this paragraph. Return is then
====== pressed.
====== __
======
======
======   When the return is pressed, three blank lines will appear
====== before this paragraph. The cursor is placed at the first new
====== line. Once the new blank lines are inserted, you may type text
====== onto them.
====== * * * END OF FILE * * *

===>
                                             X E D I T   1   FILE

7.3 Deleting Lines

To delete lines from a file, follow the same procedure for inserting new lines. However, type the letter D on the prefix area of each
line you wish to delete. These lines will disappear from the screen.


```
SAMPLE    FILE    A1    F    80    TRUNC=80 SIZE=8 LINE=0 COLUMN=1

====== * * * TOP OF FILE * * *
       |...+....1....+....2....+....3....+....4....+....5....+....6...
======    This is a sample text file.  Existing lines will be deleted
====== within this paragraph with the DELETE command.  D is typed on
D===== the prefix area of each line to delete.  Return is then
D===== pressed.
D=====
D=====
D=====
======    When the return is pressed, the lines with Ds on them will
====== disappear.   The cursor is placed at the first line after the
====== deletion.
====== * * * END OF FILE * * *



===>
                                        X E D I T   1  FILE
```

After the ENTER key is pressed, the changed file looks like this:

```
SAMPLE    FILE    A1    F    80    TRUNC=80 SIZE=4 LINE=0 COLUMN=1

====== * * * TOP OF FILE * * *
       |...+....1....+....2....+....3....+....4....+....5....+....6...
======    This is a sample text file.  Existing lines will be deleted
====== within this paragraph with the DELETE command.  D is typed on . . .
======    When the return is pressed, the lines with Ds on them
====== will disappear.   The cursor is placed at the first line after
====== the deletion.
====== * * * END OF FILE * * *



===>
                                        X E D I T   1  FILE
```

7.4 XEDIT Commands

There are several useful commands which may be used in XEDIT. These commands are all to be typed on the command line (NOT IN THE BODY OF THE PROGRAM) which is found at the bottom left of the screen (===>).

U and D - By typing in the letters U (for UP) and D (for DOWN) followed by a desired number of lines, you will be able to see up or down in the file by the number of lines specified. For example, by typing in U3 (on the command line) and hitting the "enter" key, the screen will shift so you will be able to see up three lines in the file.

You may also move forward through the file screen by screen (from beginning to end) by pressing either the Pg Dn or F8 key repeatedly. Moving backward screen by screen is accomplished by pressing either the Pg Up or F7 key.

TOP - By typing this command the screen will automatically shift to the top of the file.

BOT - By typing this command the screen will automatically shift to the bottom of the file.

QUIT - This command will exit you from XEDIT if you have not made any changes, additions, or deletions to the file you called up. Pressing the F3 key performs the same function.

QQ - If for any reason you have made changes to a program that you do not want to save, drop to the command line and type QQ (QQuit). You will exit XEDIT and your program will be as it was before you began making changes. If you attempt to exit XEDIT using QUIT (one Q) or pressing the F3 key without saving a file that has been changed, you will receive the message:

FILE HAS BEEN CHANGED.   USE QQUIT TO QUIT ANYWAY

which indicates that if you really do want to abandon the file and not save any changes, use the QQ command.

SAVE - SAVES the file you are currently editing. See below.

FILE - SAVES the file you are currently editing and exits XEDIT. See below.

7.5   Saving Changes You Make To A Program

There are two commands (SAVE and FILE) for saving changes you make to a program.   They are very similar but used for different reasons. The Save command saves changes you make to a program but leaves you in XEDIT while the FILE command saves and exits XEDIT.   When you file a program you end up back in the directory of files (if that is where you entered XEDIT from).

You will use the SAVE command only if you wish to intermittently save changes you are making to a program.   Let's suppose you are writing a large program from scratch and you are worried about the computer crashing (which would cause you to lose any unsaved portions of your program).   You would drop down to the command line periodically (by hitting the "enter" key once or twice) and type in the command SAVE.   This will save everything that has been entered into the file up to this point, including the changes just made, and leave you in the program. (You could use the FILE command for this purpose but it would take you out of XEDIT into your directory of files each time you issue the command.)

Most often you will use the FILE command. The amount of editing you will do to programs is quite minimal and the computer rarely crashes. As previously mentioned, you will issue the FILE command on the command line to save changes and exit XEDIT. The FILE command is also quite useful if you want to make a slightly modified version of an already existing program. Suppose you already have a program called RCAFREQ SAS A which gives the frequency distribution of the variables for the first assignment, the RCA case. You want to leave this program intact, but wish to create another separate program to do some simple regression analysis. You will, therefore, want to use most of the RCAFREQ SAS A program (particularly the DATA step).

Go into RCAFREQ SAS A using XEDIT. On the command line type FILE RCAREGR SAS A and hit the "enter" key. This will save the RCAFREQ file under a new name and leave RCAFREQ SAS A intact. You may now modify your new file, RCAREGR SAS A, for regression analysis. (I subjectively chose the name, RCAREGR. You may give any eight letter FILENAME you desire. You must, however, use the SAS filetype and the A filemode.)

8. THE BROWSE MODE

The browse mode is a utility to look at (not edit) a file on the screen. There are two ways of looking at a file with BROWSE. They are similar to the two methods which may be used for XEDIT. The difference for the first method is that you use the word BROWSE instead of the letter X at the CMS ready prompt. For the second and suggested method use the F2 key instead of the F4 key while looking at the directory (FLIST) of files.

There are many useful commands for the BROWSE utility. These commands must be typed in on the command line (as in XEDIT) which is now located at the top of the screen. I will mention only several relevant and needed commands.

The same directional commands used in XEDIT work with BROWSE. To go to the top (beginning) of the file use TOP. To go to the end, use BOT. U and D will move the screen Up and Down, respectively. F7 and F8 may be used instead of U and D, respectively.

In addition to the four commands: TOP, BOT U, and D, there are two others that are needed. L (followed by a desired number) and R (followed by a desired number) allows you to see those portions of a file which are off the screen to the left and/or to the right. The desired number you select refers to the number of characters you wish to move to the right or left.

The BROWSE Screen

SAMPLE   FILE   A1   F   80   1 BLK 86/01/03 LINE 1 OF 16

===>   BROWSE

This is a sample text file being viewed with BROWSE. You know you
are in BROWSE mode because the screen says so on the upper right corner
of the screen. Note that the command line is at the TOP of the screen,
unlike XEDIT, where it is at the bottom.

The BROWSE screen displays the first 20 or so lines of whatever
file you called into BROWSE with F2 (from the FLIST screen) or with the
BROWSE command.

If you need to see more of the file than is on the screen, use the
UP, DOWN, LEFT, and RIGHT commands to move the screen to the part of the
text that you want to see.

REMEMBER: In BROWSE, you can only look at a file, you CANNOT change
it.
* * * END OF FILE * * *

9. SAS

SAS (Statistical Analysis System) can execute an amazing amount of data processing commands, very quickly, if you take time to learn the basics of the system. In general, you will be writing SAS programs with XEDIT and then executing them (at the CMS prompt "R; T=0.01/0.01") by typing:

SAS FILENAME

Your SAS program will be executed "in batch" and two files will be recorded to your directory:

FILENAME SASLOG A1

-- will contain the procedure and problems SAS encountered in executing your program

FILENAME LISTING A1

-- will contain the results or "output" of you program. If your directory runs out of space to fit the listing, then you will only get the results up to the point you ran out of space. Be sure to periodically clean junk files (old LISTINGs and SASLOGs, especially) out of your directory to avoid this problem. To do this, use the ERASE command, described on pages 81 and 87.

9.1 General SAS Rules

SAS statements must end with a semicolon (;). Usually you will write one statement to a line, but several statements can be placed on one line or one statement can go on several consecutive lines.

Examples: DATA; INFILE RCA; INPUT DOG 1 CAT 2;

or

DATA;
INFILE RCA;
INPUT DOG 1 CAT 2;

SAS names can be up to 8 alphanumeric characters long. The first character must be a letter (A, B, C, ...) or underscore (_). No blanks or special characters are allowed (#, --, $, etc.).

Examples: DOG
BLUE_CAT
A235_2
FV_TV

SAS programs are made up of DATA steps and/or PROC (procedure) steps. Any number of each may be used in any one program. In the SAS programs that you will be using, all PROC steps come after the DATA step which defines the data (variable names, and so forth) for use by these subsequent PROCS. (See the RCA example, following, for a discussion of the contents of a SAS program.)

9.2   The RCA Example

OPTIONS PS = 60 LS = 80;

CMS FI GREEN DISK RCA DAT D;

DATA;
INFILE GREEN;

```
INPUT P_VD 1 P_RCA 2 I_PAST 3 I_FUTR 4 C 5
A_PRICE 6 A_FEATR 7 A_NAME 8 A_MOVIE 9 B_PRICE 10
B_FEATR 11 B_STOP 12 B_RECRD 13 B_RPRICE 14
W_PRICE 15 W_FEATR 16 W_NAME 17 W_MOVIE 18
F_FRND 19 F_TV 20 F_TVAD 21 F_SVC 22 F_CHLD 23
F_CR 24 F_MAGZN 25 I_RCA 26;
```

This is the beginning of a SAS program to analyze the RCA data.

The first line of the program defines the number of lines to be

printed on each page of the output and the maximum length of each line:

PS = 60 means page size is 60: each page has 60 lines on it.

LS = 80 means line size is 80: each line can be up to 132 characters.

(NOTE: Each physical page has a maximum of 66 lines on it, and 132
characters across. To make output from SAS easily readable on a CRT
screen, set LS=80).

The next line of the program,

CMS FI GREEN DISK RCA DAT D;

tells the computer where the data is located. This is known as a file
definition statement. The components of this statement are:

CMS   Alerts SAS to pass this statement to the main operat-
                    ing system, CMS.

FI   is short for FIle definition.

GREEN   is a randomly selected SAS name (DDname of less than 8
                    characters) which refers to the raw data file, RCA
                    DAT.

DISK   tells SAS that the raw data is on disk.

RCA DAT D   is the name of the raw data file. The file is located
                    on the D-disk.

The next line, DATA; is the command to tell SAS to create a new

(to SAS) data set. All subsequent lines of any SAS program are part of

the data step until a PROC (procedure) statement is reached. Therefore every other line that you see in the above program is part of the data step. There are no PROC statements in the program. The program only creates a (temporary) SAS data set from a raw input file. To create a permanent SAS data set, stored on your A-disk, follow the word DATA with a two-part name, the parts separated by a period (.) (e.g., DATA RCA.SASDAT;). Each part of the two-part name is of your own choosing. You use the name if you wish to have SAS use this dataset in other SAS programs without having to recreate the data set from the raw input data.

Note that all SAS statements end with a semicolon (;). A statement may be broken up over several lines, with a semicolon at the end of the last line. You may put several SAS statements on one physical line of your program so long as each ends with a semicolon.

9.3 DATA Step Statements

The INFILE statement tells the system to activate, or bring in, the raw data file indicated by the name that follows the word INFILE (GREEN in our RCA example). GREEN refers back to the File Definition statement which told CMS, the operating system, where to find RCA DAT D (on the D disk). GREEN is not an offical SAS command word. Any name could have been chosen, as long as it appeared in both the INFILE and the CMS FI statements.

The most important statement in the DATA step is the INPUT statement. INPUT tells SAS what the variable names will be and where the data for each variable is located on each line in a data file. Notice that there are no semicolons at the end of the lines of the program in the INPUT statement. That's because we want SAS to read the entire INPUT statement (including all variables) as one line. The semicolon appears only at the end of the list of all variables. If you omit a necessary semicolon anywhere in the program, there will be an error when you later try to run the program.

The INPUT statement must match the physical organization of the raw data file that it reads. Each variable is given a name (descriptive of its contents if possible), and these names are listed following the word INPUT in the same order as the data was entered on each line of the raw data file. Thus the data for question one would be the first column of the raw input file. P_VD is the name chosen for this question/variable. Since it is the first column of the raw data file, it is listed first after INPUT.

P_RCA is the variable corresponding to the answer to the second question on the questionnaire. The data for this answer is located in the second column of the raw data file, RCA DAT D. P_RCA is entered after P_VD on the INPUT statement.

The numbers that follow each variable name on the INPUT statement indicate to SAS in which column(s) of each line in the raw data file the data for the variable will be found. Thus, P_RCA is followed by a 2, indicating that the data for P_RCA will be in column 2 of each line in RCA DAT D.

Underneath the INPUT statement (still in the DATA step) you will want to create any new variables you might need. You do this simply by typing a line into the program similar to either of the following (one is for addition of variables, the second is for multiplication):

```
B = B_PRICE + B_STOP + B_RECRD + B_RPRICE;
WA_FEATR = A_FEATR * W_FEATR;
```

You will create any and all new variables in this fashion. Remember, these variable creation lines come after the INPUT statement but before any PROC statements. New variables can be created only from those variables found in the INPUT statement or from other new variables created on lines physically above in the program.

Once you have written the lines creating your new variables, you will be ready to run some procedures (PROCS) on these variables. Procedures are described in the next section.

9.4 SAS PROCedure Statements

REMEMBER THAT PROC STATEMENTS COME AFTER DATA STEPS. REMEMBER THAT DATA STEPS INCLUDE THE INFILE AND INPUT STATEMENTS, (described on pages 104-105.) AS WELL AS ANY OTHER VARIABLE CREATION LINES YOU MIGHT HAVE TYPED IN.

PROC FREQ;   By typing this into a line on your program after your
                  DATA step, you will get a frequency distribution.

PROC MEANS;   This will give the means of all the variables in the
                  data set.

PROC CORR;   This will give a correlation matrix for all the
                  variables in the data set. To get a matrix for only
                  selected variables, specify these variables in a VAR
                  statement directly beneath the PROC CORR; statement.

                  VAR (list of variables);

(NOTE: The parentheses in the VAR statement and any subsequent parentheses in these instructions are not to be included in the program.)

For Example: To get correlation coefficients for the variables P_VD, P_RCA, B_PRICE to B_RPRICE, F_CR and F_TVAD, using the RCA Video Data, we would use the following SAS program (with PROC CORR; and a VAR statement added at the end):

```
OPTIONS PS = 60 LS = 80;                        <=========
CMS FI GREEN DISK RCA DAT D;                          | |
                                                      | |
DATA;                                                 | |
INFILE GREEN;                                         | |
                                                      | |
INPUT P_VD 1 P_RCA 2 I_PAST 3 I_FUTR 4 C 5            | |
A_PRICE 6 A_FEATR 7 A_NAME 8 A_MOVIE 9 B_PRICE 10     | |    DATA
B_FEATR 11 B_STOP 12 B_RECRD 13 B_RPRICE 14           | |
W_PRICE 15 W_FEATR 16 W_NAME 17 W_MOVIE 18            | |    STEP
F_FRND 19 F_TV 20 F_TVAD 21 F_SVC 22 F_CHLD 23        | |
F_CR 24 F_MAGZN 25 I_RCA 26;                          | |    (original)
                                                      | |
WA_FEATR = A_FEATR * W_FEATR;                         | |
WA_NAME = A_NAME * W_NAME;                            | |
F = F_CR + F_CHLD + F_TVAD;                      <=========


PROC CORR;                                       <=========
    VAR P_VD P_RCA B_PRICE TO B_RPRICE                | |    PROC CORR
        F_CR  F_TVAD;                            <=========   (added)
```

PROC STEPWISE;
     MODEL (dependent {caused} variable = independent {causal} vari-
     ables) / MAXR STEPWISE;

               These two lines will generate STEPWISE REGRESSION
               output. The MAXR subcommand instructs SAS to find that
               combination of independent variables which maximize R
               squared.

PROC REG SIMPLE;
     MODEL (dependent variable = independent variable) / STB;

               Again, you shouldn't include the parentheses in the
               MODEL statement. These two lines will generate the
               simple Beta coefficients. The STB option after the
               slash requests standardized Betas of SAS. As you will
               learn in the course, you want standardized Betas for the
               CDM model.

PROC REG;
     MODEL (dependent variable = independent variables) / STB;

               These two lines generate multiple regression standard-
               ized Beta coefficients. As with the STEPWISE procedure,
               the independent variables should be entered in succes-
               sion with a space between each variable.

PROC FASTCLUS MAXCLUSTERS = N OUT = (name);
     VAR (list of variables);

               You will want to use this clustering procedure to define
               segments by demographic variables. You must specify the
               number of clusters you want in the MAXCLUSTERS option.
               (This is a subjective judgement you will have to make
               based on the size of the clusters and how distinct each
               segment is according to various demographic variables.)
               You might want to include in your list of variables,
               some or all of the demographic variables along with your
               overall A or I variable to see which segment has the
               highest Attitude or Intention. (See the discussion in
               section 10 to learn more about Segmentation Analysis.)
               (name) is the name you wish to assign to the output
               dataset of clusters, e.g., CLU1. PROC FASTCLUS
               MAXCLUSTERS = 3 OUT = CLU1; VAR I AGE INC FAMILY ED;

PROC ANOVA;
     CLASS (group variable);
     MODEL (dependent variable(s) = independent variable(s));

               We will be using the ANOVA procedure and in particular
               the F statistic to see whether or not there are

110

statistically significant differences between the
various segments that are found from Cluster Analysis.
(See the discussion in section 10 to learn more about
Segmentation Analysis.)

```
PROC ANOVA
    CLASS CLUSTER;
    MODEL I AGE INC FAMILY ED = CLUSTER;
```

NOTE: YOU MAY ONLY USE ONE MODEL STATEMENT PER PROCEDURE.

For Example: To run a regression using the Volkswagen data (WINPT
               SAS) with dependent variable BW_KNOW and independent
               variables: W_FUN, W_PRICE, W_RESAL, FW_RESAL and W_GAS
               and also printing the standardized betas, You would add
               the following PROC REG:

```
OPTIONS PS = 60 LS = 132;                              <==============
CMS FI BLUE DISK VGEN DAT D;                                        ||
FI ORANGE DISK VVOLK DAT D;                                         ||
                                                                    ||
DATA;                                                               ||
INFILE BLUE;                                                        ||
INPUT I_CLASS1 1 I_CLASS2 2                                         ||
A_FIRST 3 A_SECOND 4 A_THIRD 5 BOUGHT 6                             ||
W_RESAL 7 W_GAS 8 W_VALUE 9 W_APPER 10                              ||    DATA
W_FUN 11 W_MAINT 12 W_RELY 13 W_ACCEL 14 W_PRICE 15                 ||
W_FEATR 16 F_FIRST 17 F_SECND 18 F_THIRD 19                         ||    STEP
FM_TV 20 FM_RADIO 21 FM_NEWS 22 FM_MAGZN 23 FM_BILBD 24             ||
FV_TV 25 FV_RADIO 26 FV_NEWS 27 FV_MAGZN 28 FV_BILBD 29             ||    (original
TV_CS 30 TV_GG 31 TV 32                                             ||     WINPT
SAS)                                                                ||
TV_BNZA 33 TV_FBI 34 SEX 35 AGE 36 INC 37 ED 38;                   ||
                                                                    ||
INFILE ORANGE;                                                      ||
INPUT BW_KNOW 1 AW_LIKE 2 IW 3 CW 4                                 ||
FW_RESAL 5 FW_GAS 6 FW_VALUE 7 FW_APPER 8 FW_FUN 9                  ||
FW_MAINT 10 FW_RELY 11 FW_ACCEL 12 FW_PRICE 13 FW_FEATR 14 ||
AW_RESAL 15 AW_GAS 16 AW_VALUE 17 AW_APPER 18 AW_FUN 19             ||
AW_MAINT 20 AW_RELY 21 AW_ACCEL 22 AW_PRICE 23 AW_FEATR 24 ||
BW_GAS 25 BW_PRICE 26 BW_STYLE 27;                     <=========

PROC REG;                                              <========= PROC REG
    MODEL BW_KNOW = W_FUN  W_PRICE  W_RESAL FW_RESAL            ||
                    W_GAS / STB;                       <=========  (added)
```

10. SEGMENTATION ANALYSIS USING THE FASTCLUS PROCEDURE[1]

You were not required or able to do segmentation analysis for the first assignment, the RCA case in QE I. We will, therefore, discuss a procedure for finding segments in terms of the second case, Leanstrips. You will be using the FASTCLUS procedure described in section 9.4.

In segmentation analysis you will have to take two major decisions based on the statistical outputs. These decisions are about (a) the variables that discriminate among the segments and so can serve as the basis of segmentation as described in Chapter 15 of the text, and (b) the number of segments that you think you should divide the market into. Do not include nominal data variables because they cannot be ordered.

Start the analysis with a tentative number of segments and a list of variables which you think are important for segmentation. This number and the list will be updated several times in the course of analysis before final decisions are reached. Thus it is a trial and error procedure and subjectivity will play an important role. It is said that carrying out a good segmentation analysis is an art and the statistics merely guide this decision-making process.

The steps involved in segmentation analysis are given below:

1. Choose the variables to be used in the analysis as the basis of segmentation as described in Chapter 15 of the text. These vari-

---

1   We are indebted to Margaret Blackwood Allen for the creative work
     in rewriting this section.

ables can be attitudinal, such as attitude or intention, or behavioral, such as purchase. For example, if we want to study if INTENTION to purchase varies accross segments, INTENTION is our basic variable. INTENTION probably gives you the most dependable basis for clustering.

2. Decide on the variables which you think are good <u>descriptors</u> of the segments as described in Chapter 15. These are usually demographic variables like sex, age, and income. This is a tentative decision. If the analysis indicates that the variables included in the analysis are not significant, then you will have the option to delete these or add some other variables and rerun the analysis later.

3. Decide on the tentative number of clusters (e.g., n=3) that you want to divide the population into. Run the FASTCLUS procedure with the variables in 1) and 2) and the current value of n (number of clusters desired). Later on, FASTCLUS will be run again with different values of n and you will choose the n you think is best. (See FASTCLUS commands on p. 108.)

4. The outputs that are obtained from each run of FASTCLUS are:

   (i) The table of initial seeds.

   (ii) The table of means of segmentation variables for each cluster.

   (iii) The table of statistics of significance for each segmentation variable.

   (iv) Statistics of overall significance of the model.

The statistics in (iv) are the pseudo-F-statistic, R-squared statistic, and the cubic clustering coefficient. These three variables

113

tend to behave similarly with the number of clusters. Hence, we will base our decisions about the number of clusters on the overall R-squared statistic alone.

We need not be concerned with the initial seeds table. This just gives some technical information. In fact, this table gives the first n data points from our data file. The table of means is important but we will come to it later on. We will not deal with table (iii), the segmentation variables statistical summary. It is a better idea to use an ANOVA analysis than use table (iii) to examine if the descriptor variables are significant. Thus our decision will depend on the overall R-squared value. Note the values of n (number of clusters) and R-squared for each FASTCLUS that you run.

5.   Keep the same segmentation variables as in steps 1 and 2. Repeat steps 3 and 4 with different values of n (e.g., 4, 5, 6, 7 ...).

6.   Draw a graph of R-squared vs. n. It should look like the one below on the left.

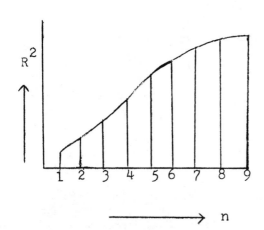

n	R^2	% improvement
1		
2		
3		
4		
5		

Complete the table on the right, above. Look at the column of percentage improvement in R-squared for addition of an extra cluster. If this is less than 10 percent (of the previous R-squared) for a particular value of n, you can conclude that this n is a reasonable number of clusters to form from your sample.

7.   Now run an ANOVA procedure to examine if the descriptor variables that have been (tentatively) selected are significant (i.e., whether they really discriminate among the clusters). Some of the variables may turn out to be insignificant. Significance is determined by reading the "F" statistic (the larger the F, the better) from the ANOVA chart for that variable. Drop the insignificant variable(s); and add any other variable(s) that you think is(are) important but had not included before. Run the FASTCLUS procedure again (steps 3 through 7, pp. 110-113) with the new list of variables. The decision about n may have to be changed because of the new or dropped variables. (See Anova commands on p. 108, additional example on p. 109.)

8.   The analysis is complete once you think that n and the list of variables need not be changed any further. As a result of this segmentation analysis, you will be able to tell which segments have the highest attitude and intention to buy. You will also be able to describe these segments in terms of demographics relative to one another and know their frequency of occurrence in the population surveyed. Now look into the table of means of segmentation variables for the final run of FASTCLUS and decide on the marketing strategy for each segment. You may decide to run the MEANS procedure (on all variables) by cluster to get a good idea about the segment profiles.

You may also decide to run the REGRESSION procedure by cluster for the CDM model.

What you now know is whether or not there is a statistically significant difference between all of your clusters taken together.

CLUSTER SIGNIFICANCE: CLUSTERS CAN BE ELIMINATED ON BASIS OR INSIGNIFICANT OR UNDESIRABLE "A" OR "I" VALUES. WE ONLY WANT TO TARGET THOSE SEGMENTS HAVING THE MOST FAVORABLE ATTITUDE OR GREATEST INTENT TO PURCHASE OUR PRODUCT. To determine which segments are desirable, examine the output data from your final FASTCLUS procedure under the column "cluster means." The segments with the most favorable I or A values (depending on which key variable was selected) are the segments to retain; all others may be deleted by the method stated below under "CLUSTER ELIMINATION PROCEDURE."

CLUSTER ELIMINATION PROCEDURE: You may want to eliminate certain meaningless clusters from the analysis. You do this by inserting a DATA step between the PROC FASTCLUS and PROC ANOVA.

Below is a sample segmentation procedural setup. I have selected 3 clusters and then have chosen to eliminate the third cluster from the ANOVA analysis.

```
PROC FASTCLUS MAXCLUSTERS = 3 OUT = clu1;
  VAR I AGE INC FAMILY ED;

DATA;
  SET clu1;
  IF CLUSTER = 3 THEN DELETE;
      (Note: if more than one cluster is to be deleted, a separate
      statement "IF CLUSTER..." must be inserted for each deletable
      cluster.)

PROC ANOVA;
```

116

```
CLASS CLUSTER;
MODEL I AGE INC FAMILY ED = CLUSTER;
```

9.   <u>RUNNING THE CDM BY CLUSTER</u>: For something extra, you may now backtrack and develop separate CDM models for each segment. This is a fairly easy procedure. You must use the editing tools you learned earlier.

A.   You may eliminate the ANOVA procedure from your segmentation procedural program.

B.   Add a PROC SORT to sort your FASTCLUS dataset (CLU1) by CLUSTER, which will place all cases together by segment:

```
PROC SORT DATA=CLU1; BY CLUSTER;
```

See p. 117 for an example. The statement must come between the FASTCLUS and data steps, as shown.

C.   Use the XEDIT editing techniques to add in the various Regression procedures from earlier programs and position them beneath the DATA step (which comes after the FASTCLUS procedure.)

D.   By adding an additional line to each of your Regression procedures you may get the regression coefficients for each cluster. After each Regression procedure model statement, add the following line:

```
BY CLUSTER;
```
                                    See p. 117 for an example.

117

This will give a separate analysis for each cluster in the output. You now have all the information you need to construct separate CDM models for each segment.

A complete SAS example, using the LEANINPT SAS program, follows:

```
OPTIONS PS = 60 LS = 132;                              <==========
CMS FI YELLOW DISK LEAN DAT A;                          ||
                                                        ||
                                                        ||
DATA;                                                   ||
INFILE YELLOW;                                          || Data
INPUT W_ADS 1 W_COST 2 W_TASTE 3 W_CONV 4 W_NUTR 5 W_NATR 6 ||
W_CHOL 7 HEARD 8 F_TV 9 F_NEWS 10 F_OTHER 11 F_ALONE 12 || Step
FR_FAV 13 FR_UNFAV 14 FR_FACTS 15 FR_EVAL 16 FR_I 17    ||
FR_TOTAL 18 FT_FAV 19 FT_UNFAV 20 FT_FACTS 21 FT_EVAL 22 ||(original)
FT_I 23 FT_TOTAL 24 F_SPEAK 25 FS_HUSB 26 FS_CHILD 27   ||
FS_REL 28 FS_FRND 29 FS_WORK 30 FS_OTHR 31              ||
F_HEAR 32 FH_HUSB 33 FH_CHILD 34 FH_REL 35 FH_FRND 36   ||
FH_WORK 37 FH_OTHR 38 F_COUPON 39 F_STORE 40 P_EVER 41  ||
P_TIMES 42 S_EAT 43 SE_HUSB 44 SE_CHILD 45 SE_OTHR 46   ||
S_SELF 47 S_FAMILY 48 P_BEFORE 49 P_AFTER 50            ||
B_BOX 51 B_PICT 52 B_SIZE 53 B_COPY 54                  ||
A_TASTE 55 A_CONV 56 A_NUTR 57 A_NATR 58 A_COST1 59     ||
A_CHOL 60 A_COST2 61 A_LIKE 62                          ||
C 63 I 64 BACON 65-66 FAMILY 67 WORK 68 H_WORK 69 ED 70 ||
AGE 71 INC 72;                                         <==========

PROC FASTCLUS MAXCLUSTERS = 3 OUT= CLU1;              <=== Segmentation PROC
     VAR I AGE INC FAMILY ED ;

PROC SORT  DATA=CLU1; BY CLUSTER;                     <=== Sorting by cluster

DATA;                                                 <====== Eliminate
  SET CLU1;                                            || meaningless
  IF CLUSTER = 3 THEN DELETE;                          || cluster (#3)


                                                      <======

PROC REG;                                             <======
  MODEL  W_TASTE = W_COST W_ADS / STB;                 || CDM
  BY CLUSTER;                                          || Regression
                                                       || PROCs
PROC REG;                                              || run by
  MODEL  FR_FAV = FR_FACTS FR_EVAL / STB;              || cluster
  BY CLUSTER;                                         <======
```

11. A NOTE ON SCALE REVERSAL

While analyzing data, it sometimes becomes necessary to reverse the order in which the responses have been coded. This is important especially (1) when responses are being combined from several questions to obtain a composite measure of a construct (as in attitude measurement), (2) when some of the questions refer to certain positive aspects of the construct while others pertain to negative ones. An example will make these points clear. Question 20 in the Leanstrips questionnaire gives a measure of attitude (the constuct under consideration). However, we find that parts A, C, E, G, and H of this question give a positive measurement of consumer attitude, while parts B, D, and F refer to negative components of attitude. Hence, before combining responses to parts A through F, we will have to reverse the scales of questions B, D, and F.

This is done as follows. Assume that a 5 point scale is to be reversed. If a consumer's actual reponse is 5 before proceeding with the analysis, we will have to recode it as 1, and so on:

Q20B Scale
(Variable A_CONV)

5	4	3	2	1	(before reversal)
1	2	3	4	5	(after reversal)

The procedure to do the recoding with SAS is to include a command similar to the one given below:

A_CONV1 = 6 - A_CONV

where A_CONV1 is a new variable. If the variable that is to be scale reversed had an n-point scale, replace the 6 in the above statement with n+1. This statement should follow the list of variables on the INPUT statement. The analysis conducted on the data should specify the new variable, A_CONV1, rather than A_CONV

In general then, to reverse scale a variable follow these steps:

1. Determine the variable to be reverse scaled.

2. Determine the range of responses possible for the variable (e.g., 1 through 7).

3. Include a statement after the INPUT statement in your SAS program creating a new variable that is a reverse scaling of the original variable:

NEW_VAR = 8 - OLD_VAR ;

Where: NEW_VAR is the name given to the new variable created by reverse scaling.

OLD_VAR is the name of the old variable that is to be reverse scaled.

8 is one plus the maximum value of the scale of OLD_VAR (e.g., 1 + 7, if OLD_VAR can range from 1 to 7)

4. Use this new variable in any statistical procedures that require a reverse scaled version of the original variable, such as combining it with other variables that were originally scaled in the opposite direction.

12. LIST OF DATA FILES AND SAS PROGRAMS FOR THE COURSE

Data File	Description	SAS Program File
RCA DAT D	All RCA Data	RCAINPT SAS D
LEAN DAT D	Leanstrips Q-1 to Q-15	LEANINPT SAS D
VGEN DAT D	General Vega Questionnaire Data	[data is accessed by the three individual programs listed below]
VVEGA DAT D	Vega Data	VINPT SAS D
VMAV DAT D	Maverick Data	MINPT SAS D
VVOLK DAT D	Volkswagen Data	WINPT SAS D
MERRILL DAT D	Cash Management Data	MLINPT SAS D
SLAMEX DAT D	Financial Management Data	SLINPT SAS D
CITIBK DAT D	Active Asset Data	CBINPT SAS D
DEANW DAT D	Focus Data	DWINPT SAS D

13. OTHER DOCUMENTATION

SAS is an extensive system with many features, and more complex analysis techniques. If you are interested in learning more of the system, the most comprehensive books are:

1. SAS USERS GUIDE: Basics.

2. SAS USERS GUIDE: Statistics.

SAS will do everything from mailing labels to Factor Analysis. This study guide has only touched on the essential features for your course in Consumer Behavior. We have purposely picked the least complicated statements and programs to help you absorb this new "language" quickly.

RCA VIDEO CASE*

Jack Sauter, RCA's group vice president for consumer electronics,
in early 1982 was quite concerned about the future of RCA's videodisc
called SelectaVision. It was not doing nearly as well in the market as
he and others had thought it would. RCA was originally very optimistic
and expected to sell 500,000 units the first year, 1980. The 1981
sales goal was 200,000 units, but by mid-October retailers had sold only
40,000 units. He and Thornton Bradshaw, Chairman of RCA, had just
returned from a meeting with the company's 60 distributorships where
they had received an up-to-date picture of what was happening out in the
field.

Further, RCA had made a very strong commitment to SelectaVision,
both financially and in terms of reputation. For example, Business
Week (10/10/83, p. 31) reports that over a twenty-year period RCA had
invested $250 million in SelectaVision. Another estimate was $780
million in research, manufacturing, and marketing. In March, 1980, RCA
had introduced this new consumer electronic product, which plays
prerecorded material on a television set. The recommended price was
$500. Substantial new technology was involved. RCA chose the less
difficult technology, the conventional needle-in-the-groove type of
instrument. It was in contrast to the technology of a laser beam for
reading the disc that IBM and MCA were jointly developing under the
brand name

* Many of the facts here are taken from the business press. There is
  no reason to believe they are incorrect but they have not been
  verified.

124

DiscoVision. A third technology called VHD (video high density) developed by Victor Co., Japan, had entered the U.S. market in June, 1980, and one of the partners in this consortium was the General Electric Company.

None of the three technologies would record in-home. The laser beam gave substantially higher fidelity than RCA's conventional needle-in-the-groove. However, RCA was improving its technology by introducing a stereo version in June of 1982 and a deluxe stereo version with remote control in August, selling for $449.

As for specific competitors, the laser beam competition was the Magnavox Division of North American Philips Corp. and U.S. Pioneer Electronics Corp. The video high density competition was Matsushita and the Japanese Victor Co. Finally, RCA had licensed its own needle-in-the-groove technology to Hitachi, Sanyo, and Toshiba, all three of which were selling the product. There also was an industrial market especially for training aids, etc., but RCA had chosen to concentrate on the consumer market.

In a sense, the greatest competition for RCA was another category of product, the videocassette recorder (VCR). It was more expensive than the RCA SelectaVision and selling for about $1,000, but it could record in-home. Also, the production technology was improving substantially so that prices of the VCR were beginning to come down from an earlier figure of $1,300 when they were introduced in 1977.

In spite of the depressing performance in 1981 when, for example, RCA lost two-thirds of its original 8,000 dealers, in 1982 things began to look better. RCA sold more SelectaVision sets in 10 weeks than it had altogether up to that point. Pioneer Video, Inc., sold more sets of the RCA technology in two summer months than at any previous time. RCA was doing a good job of marketing, illustrated in its advertising, as you can see in Figures 1 and 2.

Also, the record sales were surprisingly much better than expected. Consumers were buying more than 30 albums a year in their first year of set ownership. Videodisc records were about half the price of the videocassette recorder tapes. Also, RCA was trying very hard to develop an effective list of titles. It had such blockbusters as "On Golden Pond" and "Superman." However, RCA was strongly opposed to pornographic programming, hard or soft. It maintained this position in spite of the fact that pornographic films were accounting for as much as half of the videocassette sales and rental volume of many dealers.

As expected in a high technology industry, prices were beginning to fall. RCA dealers cut by steps from $449 to as little as $299.

Not every consumer responded in the same way to the videodisc, as might have been expected. For example, "movie fanatics" who also owned a VCR were much more likely to buy a videodisc, expecially of the laser variety. Such people seemed to want "to get nearer" the movie and the TV picture was substantially better for a laser videodisc than for a VCR.

In early 1982, Jack Sauter wanted a better foundation upon which to proceed and, if need be, to formulate a new marketing strategy. Consequently, he had a survey done of a sample of consumers to determine their buying habits. A copy of the questionnaire is attached.

You now have access to that data. Please develop from it as best
you can a recommended strategy and, for 1983, a marketing plan for Jack
Sauter, justifying the strategy and plan as best you can.

Fig. 1

HOW TO IMPROVE YOUR SOCIAL LIFE:

If you're leaving singles bars still single, if you're getting nothing but healthy at the local health club—take heart.

With the magic of the RCA VideoDisc System, you'll have great opening lines to help you make new friends. Like. "Want me to show you my Bogart collection?" Or, "Rod Stewart? He's at my place!" Or even. "Like to come over and watch me play *Superman*?"

RCA VideoDiscs can satisfy even the most demanding women. Show *Airplane* to get things off the ground with Gloria. Use *The Godfather* to make Donna an offer she can't refuse. Mix it up with Stacey over *Stir Crazy*. Get Patty to say "yes" to *Dr. No*. RCA VideoDiscs have over 250 fantastic programs you can bring home right now. There are movies.

stereo concerts, sports, the arts—and new releases every month, so you can build quite a collection. Players start at under $300, and VideoDiscs are as low as $14.98. The System is so easy even a not-so-smooth operator can operate it—and RCA VideoDiscs play on any brand of CED videodisc player and on any TV set. But only RCA has the variety to put real magic in your social life.

And if you need a break from all your new-found popularity, have a night in with the boys to watch Muhammad Ali or *Dirty Harry*.

See your nearest RCA dealer now and find out just how much magic you can bring home. What you do after that is up to you.

Fig. 2

HOW TO PUT A LITTLE EXTRA MAGIC IN YOUR MARRIAGE:

Plump up the pillows on the sofa. Forget about the office. And think about having a magical evening. The two of you. Next to each other. Alone.

With the magic of the RCA VideoDisc System, you can get the fire burning brighter with *Some Like It Hot*. Or have a close encounter of the best kind with *Close Encounters of the Third Kind*.

In fact, RCA VideoDiscs can keep you side by side on the love-seat for hours. Have a mini-honeymoon with *California Suite*. Get away from it all with *The African Queen*. Make beautiful music together with Neil Diamond in *The Jazz Singer*. Leap for joy over a ballet like *Giselle*.

RCA VideoDiscs have over 250 fantastic programs you can bring home right now. There are movies, sports, stereo

concerts, the arts—and new releases every month, so you can build your own personal collection. Players start at under $300, and VideoDiscs are as low as $14.98. The System is so easy to operate you can do it while holding hands—and RCA VideoDiscs play over and over on any brand of CED videodisc player and on any TV set. But only RCA has the variety of programs that'll put a little more spice in your life.

Watch *Fiddler on the Roof* rather than reruns on TV. Have *Victory at Sea* instead of doldrums in the den. Or show each other *Heaven Can Wait*—after the kids are in bed.

See your nearest RCA dealer now and find out just how much magic you can bring home.

And how much it can bring to your home life.

ANALYSIS OF BUYER BEHAVIOR

R.C.A. VIDEO DISK QUESTIONNAIRE

	RCA DAT AI
	Variable
Column	Name

"Hello, I am calling from a consumer research company in New York. Have I reached the (lady/man) of the house?"

>   - If yes, continue
>   - If no, seek to get the head of household

If that is not possible, thank the person and hang up.

1. We are trying to get some of your views on home entertainment.

    a. "Have you bought video disk players in the last year?"

        (i) Yes, Score 1   (ii) No, Score 0   1   P_VD

    b. If yes: "Was the video disk player you bought an RCA model or was it some other brand?

        (i) RCA, Score 1   (ii) Not RCA, Score 0   2   P_RCA

2. If respondent answered yes to either question 1a or 1b: "When you went to the store to purchase your video disk player, how much did you intend to buy it at the time? Please use a scale where 5 represents definitely intended to purchase and 1 represents definitely did not want to purchase."

Definitely did		Definitely did		
not intend to		intend to buy		
buy	1 2 3 4 5		3	I_PAST

Otherwise, using a scale of 1 to 5 where 5 represents definitely will buy and 1 represents definitely won't buy, how likely are you to buy a video disk player in the next year?

Definitely		Definitely		
will not buy	1 2 3 4 5	will buy	4	I_FUT

3. "Thinking again about video disk players, if you
   had to buy one right now, how confident would you
   be about your ability to select one? Again, please
   use a 1 to 5 scale where 1 represents not confident
   at all and 5 represents very confident."

   Not at all   Very
   confident   1 2 3 4 5   confident   5   C

4. "Now I am going to read you a statement about the
   RCA video disk player and I want you to agree or
   disagree. The more you agree, the closer you should
   rate the statement to a 5 and the more you disagree,
   you should rate the statement a 1. Is that clear?"
   If not, go back and explain it again.

   a. The RCA video disk player is very favorably
       priced   6   A_PRICE

       Disagree   1 2 3 4 5   Agree

   b. The RCA video disk player has an excellent
       array of features   7   A_FEATR

       Disagree   1 2 3 4 5   Agree

   c. RCA makes the best brand of video disk player   8   A_NAME

       Disagree   1 2 3 4 5   Agree

   d. The RCA video disk player can play the movies
       I most like to watch   9   A_MOVIE

       Disagree   1 2 3 4 5   Agree

5. "Now, I would like to ask you some questions about
   the RCA video disk player's features. These are
   multiple choice. Please select the one answer you
   feel is correct."

   a. The advertised price of the RCA video disk
       player is

       a. $395, Score 0   c. $595, Score 0   10   B_PRICE
       b. $495, Score 1   d. $695, Score 0

b. The RCA video disk player has

   a. Fast forward,
       Score 0
   b. Rewind, Score 0
   c. Fast forward,
       rewind, Score 1
   d. None of the
       above, Score 0

   11   B_FEATR

c. The RCA video disk player has

   a. Stop action
       capability,
       Score 1
   b. Does not have
       stop action
       capability,
       Score 0

   12   B_STOP

d. The RCA video disk player can record home movies

   a. Yes, Score 0   b. No, Score 1

   13   B_RECRD

e. Record prices for the RCA disk player cost
    approximately

   a. $10, Score 0   c. $20, Score 1
   b. $15, Score 0   d. $25, Score 0

   14   B_RPRICE

6. "Thinking now about all video disk players, please
    rate the following characteristics in their impor-
    tance to you. A characteristic that you believe
    is very important should receive a 5 and one of
    little to no importance should receive a 1."

   a. Price   15   W_PRICE

       Unimportant   1 2 3 4 5   Important

   b. Feature (e.g., fast forward, rewind, stop   16   W_FEATR
               action)

       Unimportant   1 2 3 4 5   Important

   c. Brand Name   17   W_NAME

       Unimportant   1 2 3 4 5   Important

   d. Available Movies   18   W_MOVIE

       Unimportant   1 2 3 4 5   Important

130

7. Finally, I want to ask you some random questions
    about video disk players in general. You only
    need answer these questions yes or no.

    a. Do close friends of yours have a video disk   19   F_FRND
        player or VCR?

            Yes, Score 1   No, Score 0

    b. Do you have a color TV?   20   F_TV

            Yes, Score 1   No, Score 0

    c. Have you ever seen video disk players or VCRs   21   F_TVAD
        advertised either on TV or in magazines?

            Yes, Score 1   No, Score 0

    d. Have you ever discussed buying a video disk   22   F_SVC
        player or VCR with your TV service man?

            Yes, Score 1   No, Score 0

    e. Do you have children who want a VCR or video   23   F_CHLD
        disk player?

            Yes, Score 1   No, Score 0

    f. Have you read the "consumer reports" write-ups   24   F_CR
        on VCRs and video disk players?

            Yes, Score 1   No, Score 0

    g. Did you read the Time and Newsweek articles on   25   F_MAGZN
        the "coming Revolution in Home Television"?

            Yes, Score 1   No, Score 0

8. If you bought a video disk player, how likely are   26   I_RCA
    you to buy an RCA?

    Definitely will   Definitely
    not buy   1 2 3 4 5   will buy

You have now completed your first case in modeling consumer behavior. It was probably a major learning experience. You are ready to do the more advanced cases partly because of having done the RCA videodisk case but also because in the course work you have been learning more advanced theory which you can now put to work. These three remaining cases offer variety and a great range of experience.

LEAN STRIPS*

Jim Cooper pushed the chair away from his desk. Belatedly, he started to organize his papers one more time. He made a pile and placed it in his left top desk drawer. The remainder he stuffed in his brief case. It was seven-thirty and snowing. He guessed he would not be home before eight.

Jim had recently been promoted to product manager. His career reaching this point had been somewhat unusual for most product managers at General Foods. Jim had started right off in Sales and never looked back. His only hard time in Sales had been overcoming some initial shyness his first several months. Thereafter, he made quota and his bonus every year. Principally because of his sales success, he had been allowed to join the Marketing Department three years ago.

Hi marketing experience until his recent promotion had been on established mature brands. First on Log Cabin Syrup and then on Jello puddings. He had always suspected that his placement on these brands was the result of his background in Sales -- and particularly his lack of an MBA. He felt his current assignment continued the pattern, although he would set the record straight on this assignment. While he wasn't sure he could raise his new product from the dead, he was sure he could show management that he was top flight.

This note was prepared as a basis for class discussion by J. L. Howard, E. W. Wood and P. Kochhar.
Special IDA Version

* The names of the people and some other details are fictitious.

Jim's problem was Lean Strips. Lean Strips was an imitation bacon product that was floundering halfway through its six month test market in Port Wayne, Indiana. It's former product manager, John Gallagher, had recently left the firm. He had accepted a junior vice-president position at Benton Bowles Advertising Agency.

Lean Strips had been John's experimental brand for the previous 2½ years. It was principally through his skilled efforts that the project had reached test market with such alacrity. Now that John was gone, the scuttlebut was that John had hoped to pin his General Foods career on the success of this product. Since it was failing, the rumor continued, John had felt forced to leave. Jim really didn't believe these stories -- but in some ways he wished John had stayed around for another year to see this project out. Politically, John had left Jim with a pretty large decision.

Lean Strips was General Food's Prepared Foods Division's most nettlesome problem. Formally, the Division had committed $60 million for national introductory market expenses . . . pending successful trial. Sunk costs in the project amounted to $15 million already, with the test market scheduled to spend another $1.5 over the next three months.

The word that circulated around the hall, however, was that the company had tentatively agreed to fund another project with the Lean Strips funds -- some kind of new adult cereal. The official word Jim got from his boss, however, was that the project was still on -- if it could be made to succeed. Apparently, the Division Manager wanted the product to succeed even if the "top brass had lost faith."

From a recent volume and profit forecast (Exhibit I) John was able to divine that Lean Strips was supposed to account for a great deal of the Division's future revenue and profit. Specifically, John Gallagher had estimated it could produce 15% of the Division's sales and 13% of the Division's profit by year five. As Jim's boss had put it to him when giving him his new assignment, "Management has lost faith in this project, but they expect you to make it work -- or come up with a really good reason why it failed."

Lean Strips had been a dream product when it was originally conceived. It was a new technology product that represented a new category as well. As an imitation bacon product, it was jutifiably argued as having a market potential equivalent to the entire bacon market, about 1.7 billion dollars. This was very pleasing to General Foods Management because it gave them the means of penetrating the prepared meat market without having to acquire or develop a meats business on their own. Further, such a penetration of the meat market was judged as having a lower probability of antitrust response than would a head-to-head entry into the meat market.

In taking Lean Strips to market, General Foods also believed they had capitalized on the growing concern over high fat/high cholesterol diets in most Americans. There had been early hopes to extend recent Heart Association and American Medical Association endorsements of low cholesterol diets to the product. Specifically, General Foods had sought to have a labeling endorsement similar to the American Dental Association endorsement of Crest toothpaste. These unfortunately failed, as both associations had a strict policy against endorsing products or brands.

Consumer blind tests of the product were mixed. Lean Strips lost to real bacon by a significant margin in blind tests on non-users. Consumers, however, who had used the product preferred it to real bacon. Further, General Foods found that this preference increased with length of use. From these findings, it was concluded that Lean Strips was a product analogous to instant coffee, where flavor preference for this product versus real coffee had developed over time with product use. Exhibit II shows these results in more detail.

Copy development for the brand had led to many long and sometimes acrid discussions in General Foods' marketing department. The product apparently had three key benefits, while General Foods preferred advertising that emphasized only one. It had lower cholesterol levels than real bacon and thus would likely be perceived as healthier to eat, but the Food and Drug Administration would not permit it to be described as causing less cholesterol. Second, it was easier to prepare (less time and spattered less) than real bacon. Third, it was less costly. Separately, it was recognized that it's imitation label represented a significant negative that had to be overcome before housewives would try it or use it regularly.

Ultimately, agreement was formed around a "tastes like real bacon" advertising copy objective with reassurances about the product's cholesterol and preparation benefits. A testimonial execution television commercial was developed for the brand in 30- and 60-second versions. Similarly, print advertising executions stresssed the same themes. Test market versions of these are in Exhibits I, II, and III.

Test market of Lean Strips had begun in March of 1974 in Fort Wayne, Indiana, and was scheduled to continue for six months. Weekly warehouse movements of the product were to be taken over the entire six-month period. These would be tracked against Neilson data and test market objectives to determine the brand's share of the bacon market and its success versus objectives, respectively. Test market objectives were set at achieving a 40% trial rate and 10% share at the end of test market. Separately, research of buyer acceptance of the product was designed to run during and after test market to determine reasons for success or failure of the brand.

Lean Strips had behaved like a loser almost from the first day. Despite early verbal agreements to have the product placed in the meats section of supermarkets, the product had to be placed in the dairy case. State law, it seems, required its placement there owing to its composition, although this was not determined until the test market began. To cope with this change in shelving policy, Jim tried to have General Foods Sales Representatives place the product beside the egg section. The switch was particularly maddening because shelf differences often made elaborate point of sale display materials useless. Worse, spot store checks on product location found that stores tended to have the product arbitrarily placed throughout the dairy case.

Early volume reports were equally disappointing. As you see in Exhibit VI, week-four volume was at only 10% of objective, resulting in a negligible share penetration of the Fort Wayne market. Some early shelf inventories had to be removed and destroyed to cope with the slow movement, thus preventing old shelf dating from further inhibiting the product's performance. By week 12, however, the product had performed better and now stood at 60% of week 12 volume objectives. Averaging the first 12 weeks now showed the product at 36% of cumulative objective.

In instances such as this, General Foods had a policy of looking to the initial market research report to explain the slow start, position it either positively or negatively from a business standpoint and indicate what the company might expect out of the product for the remainder of the test market and long term. Consequently, the product managers had tremendous latitude in working with the Market Research Department to determine what statistical analyses were needed.

Recently, General Foods had been working with an outside consultant to try to better understand what motivated consumers to buy products. The consultant, a professor of business at Columbia University, had brought with him a simple yet powerful model of consumer behavior. Basically, it contended that buyer behavior was driven by five distinct variables: Information (general product knowledge), Brand Recognition, Confidence, Attitude, and Intention to Purchase. Since the product had received recent top management interest, Jim knew that would have to be a part of his market research analysis.

The first research results had now been compiled. Jim Cooper could now begin to understand why his product was not performing. His boss was expecting the research summary within three days. Jim knew that this report would be crucial in determining the Company's long-term view of this product, and perhaps his career with General Foods.

Be sure to include in your report on the case the following information to facilitate communicating your results.

1. Model specified in form of the CDM diagram with each construct defined and each relation shown by an arrow indicating the direction of causation.

2. Describe how each construct in the model is operationalized: which questions in the questionnaire were used to represent which variables and how each question was converted into the variable.

3. Diagram of model with respective regression coefficient shown in each relation, indicating whether the coefficient is the raw number or standardized, including the significance level of each coefficient in parentheses.

4. List of equations and showing the t-values for each question.

5. Discussion of your findings and their implications for practice at each of the major levels of management.

6. The order in which you deal with these topics is up to you. Some of the material may be put in appendices.

EXHIBIT IV

Prepared Foods Division Volume & Profit Forecast

	1973		1974		1975		1976		1977	
	Volume %	Profit %	Volume %	Profit %	Volume %	Profit %	Volume %	Profit %	Volume %	Profit %
Birdseye Frozen Vegetables	37	37	37	39	35	39	33	37	33	34
Jello Puddings	20	15	18	17	16	18	14	14	14	12
Minute Rice	26	31	25	32	22	28	20	24	19	21
Shake & Bake	12	18	14	20	14	19	13	16	12	14
Log Cabin Syrup	5	2	4	2	3	3	2	3	2	2
Stove Top Stuffing	--	(2)	1	(3)	3	(2)	6	2	5	4
Lean Strips	--	(1)	1	(7)	7	(5)	12	4	15	13
TOTAL	100	100	100	100	100	100	100	100	100	100

EXHIBIT V

Lean Strips Consumer Blind Test Results

	Non-Users			3-Month Users			6-Month Users		
	Men %	Women %	Average %	Men %	Women %	Average %	Men %	Women %	Average %
Preferred Lean Strips	16	15	15	39	42	40	42	43	42
Preferred Bacon	77	76	77	46	43	44	41	40	40
Couldn't Tell	1	1	1	--	1	1	--	1	1
No Preference	6	0	7	15	15	15	17	16	17
TOTAL	100	100	100	100	100	100	100	100	100

141

EXHIBIT VI

Lean Strips Fort Wayne Test Market
Volume and Share Tracking

	Week 1	Week 2	Week 3	Week 4	Week 5	Week 6	Week 7	Week 8	Week 9	Week 10	Week 11	Week 12	Week 26
Test Market Objectives													
Weekly Movement													
Cases	830	1660	2490	3325	4155	4995	6315	6645	7475	8310	9135	9970	21600
Dollars ($000)	14.8	29.6	44.4	59.2	74.0	88.8	103.7	118.5	183.3	148.1	162.9	177.7	385.0
Share %	.4	.8	1.2	1.5	1.9	2.3	2.7	3.1	3.4	3.8	4.2	4.6	10.0
Test Market Weekly Movement													
Cases	42	183	224	337	452	899	1768	2193	3065	3740	4659	5984	
Dollars ($000)	.7	3.3	4.0	6.0	8.1	16.0	31.4	39.0	54.5	66.6	82.9	106.5	
	--	--	--	--	.2	.4	.8	1.0	1.4	1.7	2.1	2.8	
% Objective	5	11	9	10	11	18	28	33	41	45	51	60	
Cumulative Case Objective	830	2490	4980	8305	12450	17455	23770	30415	37889	45199	55334	65304	292234
Cumulative Case Results	42	225	449	786	1238	2137	3123	6062	9127	12867	17526	23510	
% of Objective	5	9	9	9	10	12	13	20	24	29	32	36	

Interviewer _____

PC/4341 (SAS) Version

Respondent _____

1/1/87

Phone # _____

City _____

Introduction

Hello. I'm a graduate student at Columbia University, calling from New York City. May I speak to the lady of the house? (If initial contact is not lady of the house, return to "hello" when she comes to the phone.) We're conducting a survey of consumer attitudes here at the University, and I'd like to ask you a few questions.

First, do you have children living at home? (If no, explain that the survey requires mothers with children at home, thank her and hang up. If yes, proceed.)

There are no right or wrong answers in this study. The best answer is your own personal problem.

		Column	Variable Label
1.	How important to you is new food advertising, relative to all advertising. Would you say it is:	1	W-ADS

    1. not applicable
    2. very unimportant
    3. somewhat unimportant
    4. neither important nor unimportant
    5. somewhat important
    6. very important

2. When you purchase food for your family, how important are the following considerations? After I read the list of words, please tell me which is the most important (6th), the second most important, the third most important, etc., down to the 1st or least important one:

	1	2	3	4	5	6	N.A.	Column	Variable Label
Cost	__	__	__	__	__	__	__	2	W-COST
Taste	__	__	__	__	__	__	__	3	W-TASTE
Convenience	__	__	__	__	__	__	__	4	W-CONV
Nutrition	__	__	__	__	__	__	__	5	W-NUTR
Naturalness	__	__	__	__	__	__	__	6	W-NATR
Cholesterol	__	__	__	__	__	__	__	7	W-CHOL

3. Have you heard of Lean Strips? (If no, skip to question #23)

       1. No ___   2 Yes ___   8   HEARD

4. Now I will list ways you might have heard about or seen Lean Strips. After I read each one, could you tell me whether you have seen or heard about Lean Strips this way very often, often, occasionally, rarely, or never.

	Very Often	Often	Occas.	Rarely	Never		
On television	5__	4__	3__	2__	1__	9	F-TV
In the newspaper	5__	4__	3__	2__	1__	10	F-NEWS
From other people	5__	4__	3__	2__	1__	11	F-OTHR
In a store	5__	4__	3__	2__	1__	12	F-ALONE

5. What are the key points you recall from advertising for Lean Strips?

      _____   13 FR-FAV
                                              14 FR-UNFAV
      _____   15 FR-FACTS
                                              16 FR-EVAL
      _____   17 FR-I
                                              18 FR-TOTAL

Question 5 is coded as follows:

Column: 13 number of "favorable" points - good
             product features
         14 number of "unfavorable" points - bad
             product features
         15 number of "factual" points - straight
             facts recalled
         16 number of "evaluative" points -
             respondent judgment
         17 number of "intentional" points -
             respondent intention to act (there
             were none)
         18 total number of points mentioned

6. What thoughts come to mind when you think of the
    advertising for Lean Strips?

    _____   19   FR-FAV
                                                          20   FR-UNFAV
    _____   21   FR-FACTS
                                                          22   FR-EVAL
    _____   23   FR-I
                                                          24   FR-TOTAL

    Question 6 is coded as follows:

    Column: 19 number of "favorable" thoughts
             20 number of "unfavorable" thoughts
             21 number of "factual" thoughts
             22 number of "evaluative" thoughts
             23 number of "intentional" thoughts
                 (here some respondents did express
                 intentions to act)
             24 total number of thoughts mentioned

7. Have you spoken to others about Lean Strips?

            1. No ___   2. Yes ___   25   F-SPEAK

    If yes, did you speak to

        1   your husband   26   FS-HUSB
        1   your children   27   FS-CHILD
        1   relatives   28   FS-REL
        1   friends   29   FS-FRND
        1   people at work   30   FS-WORK
        1   others (who? _____)   31   DS-OTHR

	Column	Variable Label

8. Have you heard about Lean Strips from others?

        1. No ___   2. Yes ___   32   F-HEAR

   If yes, did you hear about them from:

		Column	Variable Label
1	your husband	33	FS-HUSB
1	your children	34	FS-CHILD
1	relatives	35	FS-REL
1	friends	36	FS-FRND
1	people at work	37	FS-WORK
1	others (who? _____)	38	DS-OTHR

9. Did you receive any coupons for Lean Strips?

        1. No ___   3. Yes ___   39   F-COUPON

10. Do you think that your regular food store carries   40   F-STORE
Lean Strips? Would you say that:

      5   it definitely does
      4   it probably does
      3   you are not sure one way or the other
      2   it probably does not
      1   it definitely does not

11. Have you ever purchased Lean Strips?

        1. No ___   3. Yes ___   41   P-EVER

12. On how many shopping occasions or trips to the store
did you purchase Lean Strips in the last three weeks?

        _____   42   P-TIMES

13. Did you eat Lean Strips yourself?

        1. No ___   3. Yes ___   43   S-EAT

14. Did you serve Lean Strips to:

				Column	Variable Label
1	your husband	1 No___	2 Yes___	44	SE-HUSB
2	your children	1 No___	2 Yes___	45	SE-CHILD
3	others (who? _____)			46	SE-OTHR

15. How satisfied were you with Lean Strips when you
    used them? Would you say you were: 47   S-SELF

    1   extremely dissatisfied
    2   dissatisfied
    3   indifferent
    4   satisfied
    5   extremely satisfied

16. How satisfied was your family with Lean Strips when   48   S-FAMILY
    you used them? (For each person mentioned in
    answer to #14, and using scale from #15.)

    1   extremely dissatisfied
    2   dissatisfied
    3   indifferent
    4   satisfied
    5   extremely satisfied

17. Did you buy Lean Strips before or after you saw them   49   P-BEFORE
    advertised?

    1   before
    2   after

18. Did you purchase Lean Strips before or after you   50   P-AFTER
    discussed the product with others?

    1   before
    2   after

19. (a) What kind of package does Lean Strips come in?   51   B-BOX
         (Don't read choices -- use them only to
         record responses)

    1   box
    2   other response _____
    3   don't know
    4   N.A.

    (If answered #1, "box" - received a 2 (yes),
    otherwise received a 1 (no))

   (b) What picture does the Lean Strips package show?   52   B-PICT
         (Don't read choices -- use them only to
         record responses)

1   breakfast (or bacon & eggs)
2   other response _____
3   don't know
4   N.A.

(If answered #1, "breakfast" - received a 2
(yes), otherwise received a 1 (no))

(c) Compared to a package of bacon, is the Lean   53   B-SIZE
     Strips package larger or smaller?

          1   larger
          2   smaller
          3   don't know
          4   N.A.

     (If answered #1, "smaller" - received a 2 (yes),
     otherwise received a 1 (no))

(d) Does the package say that Lean Strips should be   54   B-COPY
     frozen or refrigerated?

          1   frozen
          2   refrigerated
          3   don't know
          4   N.A.

     (If answered #2, "refrigerated" - received a 2
     (yes), otherwise received a 1 (no))

20. Now I will read a list of statements that describe
     Lean Strips. After I read each statement, please
     tell me if you strongly agree, agree, neither agree
     nor disagree, disagree, or strongly disagree with it.

		strongly agree	agree	neither	agree	strongly disagree		
(a)	Lean Strips are very delicious tasting	5	4	3	2	1	55	A-TASTE
(b)	Lean Strips are not convenient	5	4	3	2	1	56	A-CONV
(c)	Lean Strips are very nutritious	5	4	3	2	1	57	A-NUTR

							Column	Variable Label
(d)	Lean Strips are very artificial	5	4	3	2	1	58	A-NATR
(e)	Lean Strips are a good buy for the money	5	4	3	2	1	59	A-COSTL
(f)	Lean Strips are high in cholesterol	5	4	3	2	1	60	A-CHOL
(g)	Lean Strips are less expensive than bacon	5	4	3	2	1	61	A-COST2
(h)	In general, I like Lean Strips very much	5	4	3	2	1	62	A-LIKE

21. How confident are you of your ability to judge   63   C
    the quality of Lean Strips? Would you say that
    you are:

                5   extremely confident
                4   somewhat confident
                3   not sure one way or the other
                2   somewhat unconfident
                1   not confident at all

22. How likely are you to buy Lean Strips in the next   64   I
    month? Would you say you:

                5   definitely will
                4   probably will
                3   are not sure one way or the other
                2   probably will not
                1   definitely will not

23. Approximately how many times per month do you   65-66 BACON
    usually serve real bacon to your family?

    _____

24. Including yourself, what is the total number of   67   FAMILY
    people living in your household?

    _____

	Column	Variable Label

25. Are you employed outside of the home?   68   WORK

         1   full-time
         2   part-time
         3   not at all

26. What is your husband's occupation?   69   H-WORK

_____

27. What was the last grade you completed?   70   ED

1. Grade school or less   4. Some college
2. Some high school   5. Graduated from
3. Graduated from high school   college or higher

28. Please tell me which age group applies to you: 71   AGE

     1. Under 20   4. 40-49
     2. 20-29   5. 50-59
     3. 30-39   6. 60 or over

29. Which of the following categories comes closest to   72   INC
your yearly family income?

     1. Under $5,000   4. $15,000-$20,000
     2. $5,000-10,000   5. Over $20,000
     3. $10,000-15,000

THE CHEVROLET VEGA CASE

As Brad Connors, project manager of the Vega, returned to his office, he was justifiably happy with himself. He had just concluded a successful meeting with some of his Company's most important individuals. The meeting had gone well, and Brad's presentation had been complimented. He was off to a great start in his new assignment.

The meeting has consisted of Brad; John Z. DeLorean, President of the Chevrolet Division; Patrick O'Connel, Senior Vice President of Chevrolet Manufacturing; Thomas Staudt, a Senior Project Director for Chevrolet and Brad's immediate superior; Scott Conrad, Chevrolet's Marketing Director; and Bill Haley, Senior Vice President with Doyle, Dane, Inc., Chevrolet's advertising agency. The subject of the meeting was the introduction of General Motors' new subcompact car, code name XP-887, soon to be announced to the general public as the Chevrolet Vega. The date was July 15, 1970.

At issue in the meeting was the Vega's cost and pricing. Some new calculations by the Chevrolet Manufacturing Department indicated that the Vega could not be brought in on its cost target. This in turn appeared to indicate that the Vega would need to have a consumer price of $2,015 to deliver its target margin of 12% and rate of return of 15%. This cost pricing news was not pleasant to anyone at the meeting. It was an accepted fact, however, as the calculations had been run about a dozen times to verify them.

What had occurred to drive up the Vega's cost was some post-prototype engineering to give the car more structural strength. Specifically, extended testing of the Vega prototype had turned up multiple areas that Chevrolet engineers felt needed reinforcement. With such little time to introduction -- it was February when these findings were made, and production was scheduled for July for a September introduction at Chevrolet showrooms -- there was nothing to do but add more metal to the affected areas. The result was to increase the car's weight by about 200 lbs., from a planned 1,950 lbs. to 2,150 lbs. This extra steel translated into about $200 of additional cost.

Chevrolet management had agonized over these cost-increasing structural changes for several months prior to making the decision to go ahead with them. This was because they had targeted at having the Vega priced at parity with the leading import -- the Volkswagen Beetle. In making the decision, GM was placed on the horns of a dilemma. On the one hand, their prior experience with Corvair had taught them that introducing a poorly made small car could have even more disastrous results than poor sales. On the other hand, they had also watched the import market grow each year in sales and share, principally because imports were priced below competition from Detroit.

As background, the Corvair had been introduced in 1960 as GM's first import fighter. Even more than the Vega, the Corvair was an innovative car featuring a rear air-cooled engine for maintenance simplicity and superior poor-weather handling. It also had a rear-wheel independent suspension to improve its ride. However, these

152

same innovations actually caused the car to be very undependable and to have unpredictable emergency-handling characteristics. These, in turn, caught the interest of a young consumer affairs advocate named Ralph Nader. He published a book about the car, Unsafe at Any Speed. This not only led to declining sales but congressional hearings on auto safety. Thereafter, congressional interest in regulating automobile manufacturers snowballed such that by 1970 all manufacturers had to comply with a host of safety and pollution regulations. The Corvair itself was retired in 1966 as an unmitigated disaster.

Given the Corvair's lack of success, the entire American automobile industry had avoided producing import-sized small cars. Instead, Detroit focused on producing "compact" cars that were at once somewhat larger and more expensive than the imports, and which Detroit hoped American consumers would view as a better overall value. However, import sales continued to grow steadily -- from a low of 340,000 units in 1962 to 1,100,000 units by 1969. Similarly, Japanese competition, principally from Datsun and Toyota, had 1969 shipments of 470,000 units, with estimated 1970 sales of 550,000 units, having started with virutally no sales at the beginning of the decade. For a longer view, see Table 1.

Table 1 Structure of New Car Sales

Year	Size Class				
	Subcompact[a]	Compact	Intermediate	Standard	Luxury
1967	9.3	15.7	23.6	47.9	3.1
1972	22.7	15.4	21.7	36.1	3.4
1973	24.9	17.7	23.0	30.0	3.6
1974	28.4	20.0	24.2	22.6	3.7
1975	32.4	20.3	24.1	17.9	4.0
1976	26.1	23.5	27.3	19.4	3.7
1977	27.1	21.2	26.9	19.4	4.6
1978	26.4	21.6	26.8	18.4	5.5
1979	34.0	20.0	24.2	15.3	5.5
1980[b]	42.0	20.2	20.6	12.5	4.7

[a] Includes imports.
[b] January and February.

Source: NRC, The Competitive Status of the U.S. Auto Industry, National Academy Press, 1982, p. 19.

However, the American compacts, Corvair, Falcon, and Valiant easily were more successful in terms of sales. Admittedly, some of the sales came from the heavier domestic car market, but most of the gain came from foreign manufacturers except the VW Beetle, which continued to grow.

From Table 1, you obtain a clear picture of strong, growing demand for subcompacts in the U.S. in the late 1960s and especially in the 1970s. This is not surprising because the small car sales were encouraged by fundamental demographic trends such as increased urbanization, shifts in the age growth in multicar families.

The price of gas, of course, worked against the larger cars in the 1970s as you see in Figure 1.

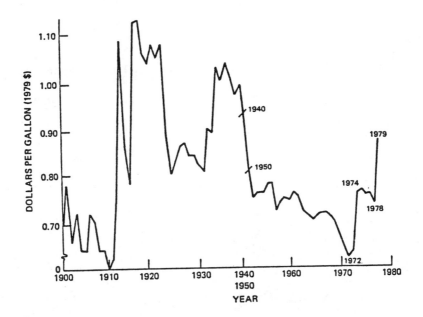

FIGURE 1 Real price of gasoline from 1900 to 1979 (in 1979 dollars).

Source: NRC, The Competitive Status of the U.S. Auto Industry, National Academy Press, 1982, p. 134.

While the Vega project had begun prior to the appointment of John Z. DeLorean as Division President of Chevrolet, he was quick to take an interest in it. More specifically, John DeLorean viewed the Vega as a means to increase Chevrolet's sales substantially -- adding approximately 500,000 units to a base of about 2,000,000 units, thus building Chevy's share of the automobile market from 30% to 35%. DeLorean argued convincingly that it would be difficult for Chevrolet to realize growth by building bigger, more luxurious cars. Pontiacs, Buicks, and Oldsmobiles had a more creditable hold on that franchise. Therefore, it was left to Chevrolet to take on the imports.

The immediate problem with taking on the imports was that they had cheaper labor and steel. Yet to be successful, the Vega must be priced comparably. Specifically, it was estimated that German and Japanese laborers made the equivalent of $3.20/hour and $2.20/hour, respectively, versus $4.30/hour for Americans. Similarly, German steel was roughly priced at parity with U.S. steel, both costing about $500/ton; whereas Japanese steel could be bought for roughly $425/ton. What this meant, according to GM estimates, is that if Americans built the same car as the Germans and the Japanese, the latter two could price under the Americans by 15% and 25%, respectively.

Meeting import labor and steel cost advantages meant that Chevrolet had to make up the difference in productivity -- making more cars per unit of time. Prior to the Vega, standard production rates for American, German, and Japanese cars were 60 cars per hour. The Vega, on the other hand, would be produced at a rate of 100 cars/hour. Theoretically, this would give the Vega a production cost lower than either the VW or comparable Japanese competition. However, even before th most recent structural reinforcements, Chevrolet engineers had insisted on making the Vega use more steel than its import competitors. Also, Chevrolet expected that autumn negotiations with the United Auto Workers would produce raises that would consume the rest of these cost efficiencies. Import and Vega pricing details are in Figure 2.

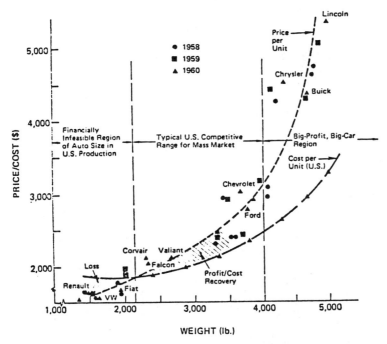

FIGURE 2 Price, cost, and vehicle size for selected models, 1958, 1959, and 1960. (From Consumer Reports, April issues, 1958, 1959, 1960.)

Source: NRC, The Competitive Status of the U.S. Auto Industry, National Academy Press, 1982, p. 69.

As Figure 2 shows us, the VW was not only a light car but was priced quite low in relation to its weight. Further, its cost was much lower than would have been an American car of the same weight.

Because of the heavy upfront investment of the Vega project -- the Vega used remarkably few components from other GM vehicles and would be produced at its own new factory -- GM wanted to maximize the number of units sold in the first year. Indeed, the first-year target for the Vega was set at 400,000 units -- fully 40% the number of units of full-sized Chevrolets and nearly equal to 1969 Volkswagen sales.

Chevrolet's strategy for achieving this goal rested on two basic tenets. First, the Vega would be introduced as a full-line automobile having sedan, hatchback, and station wagon models. Second, the Vega would run advertising designed to raise public awareness of the Vega to VW levels prior to the Vega's arrival at Chevrolet showrooms in September.

This advertising goal was particularly challenging. Specifically, market research General Motors had conducted previously showed that the VW had established an awareness level of 90% by 1969. Further, it had a recognition level -- this meant people could name it by looking at its picture -- of 66%. These awareness and recognition levels compared favorably to even Chevrolet's mid-size and compact models (90% awareness, 60% recognition) and surpassed a host of other General Motors cars -- notably, the Camaro, Firebird, and Cadillac El Dorado. Additionally, past experience with other General Motors cars showed it typically took about 3-4 years for awareness and recognition levels to reach full development.

Toward meeting the Vega's awareness and recognition goals, Chevrolet's Marketing Department and Doyle Dane decided on a heavy schedule of pre-announcement advertising starting nine months prior to introduction. The first seven months would feature print advertising only. The last two months would begin a TV blitz. The car's name would be announced once TV advertising began, but would not be named in prior advertisements. The theme selected for the campaign was to call the Vega "the little car that does everything well."

In order to facilitate comparison shopping, Vega's pre-announcement advertising would be very factual and contain much information about the performance, size, etc., of the car. Chevrolet management calculated that this would affect consumers in two important ways. First, they hoped that consumers would form a positive opinion about the Vega prior to its introduction. Second, they also hoped that many consumers would delay buying an import in the spring and summer, preferring to wait for the Vega's introduction. This would, in turn, create a pipeline of consumer demand for the Vega when it was introduced in September.

To measure the performance of this advertising campaign, GM committed to run three waves of research throughout the nine-month campaign. The first wave was scheduled to be run in May, with subsequent waves planned for August and October. By having the first two waves early on, GM would be allowed time to adjust the levels of their advertising to meet the Vega's high awareness and recognition objectives. Similarly, the third wave would measure how well they actually fared and provide data on which to improve the Vega's Year I copy and media plans. Waves 4 and 5 were January and May, 1971, respectively.

The research design had been developed in conjunction with a respected outside research firm and in consultation with three professors from Columbia University's Graduate School of Business who sought to model consumers' reactions to the Vega as it developed. The research was to be comparative in nature, seeking to measure consumers' perceptions of the Vega against the Volkswagen and the Ford Maverick. More specifically, the study would employ the same panel of respondents for each of the waves, who would be taken randomly from national lists of heads of households, aged 18 and up. Results of the study would be analyzed by Chevrolet's Marketing Department and the outside research firm.

Unfortunately, results from the first wave of research had proved unusable. Specifically, the measured awareness levels of the Vega had been nil, but the Volkswagen and the Maverick had also registered poor awareness levels -- below 40% for both -- in sharp contrast to previous research. This caused great consternation at the upper echelons of General Motors' management and resulted in the replacement of the GM research manager assigned to the project. This, in turn, had made way for Brad Connors' appointment to project manager. It also put him in a spot of high visibility within the Company.

Based on his prior experience, Brad quickly noted two problems with the Wave I research. First, many of the questions had been worded in a manner confusing to respondents, resulting in a great many "don't know" responses. Second, the telephone list used was considered a "shabby" one among the market research trade. Brad quickly worked to have the questionnaire reworded and also had a new set of respondents taken from a new, better-known telephone list.

Brad had expected his meeting with John DeLorean to be centered on these changes. The questions raised about the Vega's price at the meeting had been unexpected. He had sought to explain that market research on pricing is very hard to do in general, and the specific research fielded on the Vega was not designed to help "price" the car. Nevertheless, John DeLorean indicated that he wanted to know what the study would recommend to do with the Vega's price. Thomas Staudt had also indicated that this did not mean that the study's true purpose should be ignored either -- that of providing an analysis of the effectiveness of the Vega marketing plans to date. Brad knew he had his work cut out for him, but he relished the chance to show his ability. His report would have to make evaluations and recommendations for each of the major levels of management in General Motors, including Mr. Roche, the CEO.

To perform effectively, Brad knew that he should prepare a marketing strategy for the Vega. He needed it as a framework, both to ensure a meeting of the minds with John DeLorean and to guide his thinking in developing recommendations.

Be sure to include in your report on the case the following information to facilitate communicating your results.

1. Model specified in form of the CDM diagram with each construct defined and each relation shown by an arrow indicating the direction of causation.

2. Describe how each construct in the model is operationalized: which questions in the questionnaire were used to represent which variables and how each question was converted into the variable.

3. Diagram of model with respective regression coefficient shown in each relation, indicating whether the coefficient is the raw number or standardized, including the significance level of each coefficient in parentheses.

4. List of equations and showing the t-values for each question.

5. Discussion of your findings and their implications for practice at each of the major levels of management.

6. The order in which you deal with these topics is up to you. Some of the material may be put in appendices.

CHEVROLET VEGA QUESTIONNAIRE

1. Now, let's talk about the entire product class to
   which these new cars belong, including cars such as
   OPEL, TOYOTA, MAVERICK, and VOLKSWAGEN, as well as
   GREMLIN, VEGA 2300, and PINTO. Using a scale from
   one to nine, where one represents "definitely will
   not buy" and nine represents "definitely will buy,"
   what number represents how definite you are about
   buying one of these small economy cars within the
   next three months? (Repeat scale if necessary to be
   sure respondents understand the meaning of the
   numbers.)

   Definitely   1 2 3 4 5 6 7 8 9 Definitely   G1 I_CLASS1
   will not buy   will buy

2. Using the same one to nine scale, how definite are
   you about buying one of these models within the next
   two years?

   Definitely   1 2 3 4 5 6 7 8 9 Definitely   G2 I_CLASS2
   will not buy   will buy

   Let me ask you a few special questions about three
   of these cars. Let's discuss Volkswagen, Maverick,
   and Vega.

3. How much do you feel that you know about each of
   the automobiles, with one meaning you know nothing
   and nine meaning you know a great deal?

3a. VOLKSWAGEN
    Nothing   1 2 3 4 5 6 7 8 9 A great   W1 BW_KNOW
    at all   deal

3b. MAVERICK
    Nothing   1 2 3 4 5 6 7 8 9 A great   M1 BM_KNOW
    at all   deal

3c. VEGA
    Nothing   1 2 3 4 5 6 7 8 9 A great   V1 BV_KNOW
    at all   deal

4. Now, I would like you to give me your impression of
   each of the automobiles, rating one as disliking the
   car very much and nine as liking it very much.

4a. VOLKSWAGEN
     I dislike   1 2 3 4 5 6 7 8 9   I like   W2 AW_LIKE
     this car   this car
     very much   very much

4b. MAVERICK
     I dislike   1 2 3 4 5 6 7 8 9   I like   M2 AM_LIKE
     this car   this car
     very much   very much

4c. VEGA
     I dislike   1 2 3 4 5 6 7 8 9   I like   V2 AV_LIKE
     this car   this car
     very much   very much

4d. Please rank the three cars (Car 1, Car 2, and Car 3)
     in terms of your preference.

     Which one would be your first choice?   G3 A_FIRST

     Which would be your second choice?   G4 A_SECOND

     Interviewer: Check remaining one make as   their   G5 A_THIRD
     third choice.
                        Coding for Question 4d
                        Car   Code
                        Volkswagen   1
                        Gremlin   2
                        Vega 2300   3
                        Maverick   4
                        Toyota   5
                        Hornet   6
                        Opel   7
                        Pinto   8
                        None/Don't Know   9

     How definite are you about buying one of these particular
     automobiles in the next three months? Rating one as being
     "definitely will not buy" and 9 as "definitely will buy."

5a. VOLKSWAGEN
     Definitely   1 2 3 4 5 6 7 8 9   Definitely   W2 IW
     will not buy   will buy

5b. MAVERICK
     Definitely   1 2 3 4 5 6 7 8 9   Definitely   M2 IM
     will not buy   will buy

164

5c. VEGA
   Definitely   1 2 3 4 5 6 7 8 9 Definitely   V2 IV
   will not buy   will buy

6. How confident are you about your ability to make a
   judgment or buying decision about each of these cars
   based on the information you now have? Rate each car
   with one if you are not at all confident in your
   judgment and nine if you are very confident.

6a. VOLKSWAGEN
   Not at all   1 2 3 4 5 6 7 8 9 Very   W3 CW
   confident   confident

6b. MAVERICK
   Not at all   1 2 3 4 5 6 7 8 9 Very   M3 CM
   confident   confident

6c. VEGA
   Not at all   1 2 3 4 5 6 7 8 9 Very   V3 CV
   confident   confident

7. Have you bought a new car during the past three   G6 BOUGHT
   months?

                    0 No   1 Yes

8. For each of the cars we mentioned previously, please
   indicate if, from any source -- such as advertising,
   magazine articles, car salesmen, talking with friends
   and acquaintances, etc. -- you remember receiving any
   information during the last 30 days about each of the
   following characteristics of these small economy cars.

   For example:
   Have you heard anything about Volkswagen "resale value"
   in the last 30 days? How about Maverick "resale value"?
   How about Vega "resale value"? How about Volkswagen
   "roominess and comfort"? etc.

READ LIST AND ROTATE	COLUMN	W	M	V
Resale value	5	FW_RESAL	FM_RESAL	FV_RESAL
Gas economy	6	FW_GAS	FM_GAS	FV_GAS
Value for money	7	FW_VALUE	FM_VALUE	FV_VALUE

165

Overall exterior appearance	8	FW_APPER	FM_APPER	FV_APPER
Ease and fun of driving	9	FW_FUN	FM_FUN	FV_FUN
Simplified design for easy maintenance and serviceability	10	FW_MAINT	FM_MAINT	FV_MAINT
Reliability and quality of construction	11	FW_RELY	FM_RELY	FV_RELY
Pickup and acceleration	12	FW_ACCEL	FM_ACCEL	FV_ACCEL
Purchase price	13	FW_PRICE	FM_PRICE	FV_PRICE
Availability of features I want	14	FW_FEATR	FM_FEATR	FV_FEATR

Coding for Question 8

	Code
Yes	1
No	0

9. I would like you to tell me something about how important the factors we just talked about are in choosing a small economy car.

The less important you feel the factor is, the further toward one you should rate it, and the more important you feel the factor is, the further toward nine your evaluation should be.

As an example:
I would like to have you tell me how important or unimportant you feel "resale value" is in choosing a small economy car. What about "gas economy," etc.?

	Unimportant							Important		
Resale value	1 2 3 4 5 6 7 8 9								G7	W_RESAL
Gas economy	1 2 3 4 5 6 7 8 9								G8	W_GAS
Value for money	1 2 3 4 5 6 7 8 9								G9	W_VALUE
Overall exterior appearances	1 2 3 4 5 6 7 8 9								G10	W_APPER

Ease and fun of driving	1	2	3	4	5	6	7	8	9	G11 W_FUN
Simplified design for easy main- tenance and serviceability	1	2	3	4	5	6	7	8	9	G12 W_MAINT
Reliability and quality of construction	1	2	3	4	5	6	7	8	9	G13 W_RELY
Pickup and acceleration	1	2	3	4	5	6	7	8	9	G14 W_ACCEL
Purchase price	1	2	3	4	5	6	7	8	9	G15 W_PRICE
Availability of features I want	1	2	3	4	5	6	7	8	9	G16 W_FEATR

10. I'm going to read you a statement about each one of the three cars.

For each statement, please indicate whether you agree or disagree with the statement. The more you agree with a statement, the closer to nine you should rate it. If you disagree with a statement, you should rate it closer to one.

As an example:
Volkswagen "has high resale value." If you agree, rate it nine; if you disagree, rate it one. Pinto "has high resale value," etc.

CIRCLE ONE FOR EACH CAR

READ LIST AND ROTATE	Disagree								Agree	
Has high resale value										
Volkswagen	1	2	3	4	5	6	7	8	9	W15 AW_RESAL
Maverick	1	2	3	4	5	6	7	8	9	M15 AM_RESAL
Vega	1	2	3	4	5	6	7	8	9	V15 AV_RESAL
Excellent gas economy										
Volkswagen	1	2	3	4	5	6	7	8	9	W16 AW_GAS
Maverick	1	2	3	4	5	6	7	8	9	M16 AM_GAS
Vega	1	2	3	4	5	6	7	8	9	V16 AV_GAS

Excellent value for money

Volkswagen	1	2	3	4	5	6	7	8	9	W17	AW_VALUE
Maverick	1	2	3	4	5	6	7	8	9	M17	AM_VALUE
Vega	1	2	3	4	5	6	7	8	9	V17	AV_VALUE

Nice overall exterior appearance

Volkswagen	1	2	3	4	5	6	7	8	9	W18	AW_APPER
Maverick	1	2	3	4	5	6	7	8	9	M18	AM_APPER
Vega	1	2	3	4	5	6	7	8	9	V18	AV_APPER

Easy and fun to drive

Volkswagen	1	2	3	4	5	6	7	8	9	W19	AW_FUN
Maverick	1	2	3	4	5	6	7	8	9	M19	AM_FUN
Vega	1	2	3	4	5	6	7	8	9	V19	AV_FUN

Simplified design for easy maintenance and serviceability

Volkswagen	1	2	3	4	5	6	7	8	9	W20	AW_MAINT
Maverick	1	2	3	4	5	6	7	8	9	M20	AM_MAINT
Vega	1	2	3	4	5	6	7	8	9	V20	AV_MAINT

Is very reliable and well constructed

Volkswagen	1	2	3	4	5	6	7	8	9	W21	AW_RELY
Maverick	1	2	3	4	5	6	7	8	9	M21	AM_RELY
Vega	1	2	3	4	5	6	7	8	9	V21	AV_RELY

Has good pickup and acceleration

Volkswagen	1	2	3	4	5	6	7	8	9	W22	AW_ACCEL
Maverick	1	2	3	4	5	6	7	8	9	M22	AM_ACCEL
Vega	1	2	3	4	5	6	7	8	9	V22	AV_ACCEL

Is not expensive

Volkswagen	1	2	3	4	5	6	7	8	9	W23	AW_PRICE
Maverick	1	2	3	4	5	6	7	8	9	M23	AM_PRICE
Vega	1	2	3	4	5	6	7	8	9	V23	AV_PRICE

Has availability of features I want

Volkswagen	1	2	3	4	5	6	7	8	9	W24	AW_FEATR
Maverick	1	2	3	4	5	6	7	8	9	M24	AM_FEATR
Vega	1	2	3	4	5	6	7	8	9	V24	AV_FEATR

11. I would like to determine how much you recall about the specifications of these cars. I'll read you a characteristic, for an example, "gas economy" of the Volkswagen and you tell me whether you think it is "under 20 mpg," "20-24 mpg," "30-34 mpg," etc.

Identification Number	Volks-wagen	Maverick	Vega		
Gas Economy					
Under 20 miles per gallon	0	0	0		
20-24 miles per gallon	0	0	0	Volkswagen	W25 BW_GAS
25-29 miles per gallon	1	1	1	Maverick	M25 BM_GAS
30 miles per gallon or over	0	0	0	Vega	V25 BV_GAS
Don't know	0	0	0		

Identification Number	Volks-wagen	Maverick	Vega		
Selling Price					
Under $1,900	1	0	0		
$1,900-$1,999	0	0	0	Volkswagen	W26 BW_PRICE
$2,000-$2,099	0	1	1		
$2,100-$2,199	0	0	0	Maverick	M26 BM_PRICE
$2,200-$2,299	0	0	0		
$2,300 and over	0	0	0	Vega	V26 BV_PRICE

C. Body styles available

(Score one for each correct answer given. No correct answers gets a "0")

1. 2-door sedan		
2. 4-door sedan	Volkswagen	W27 BW_STYLE
3. 2-door sports coupe		
4. 2-door "hatchback" coupe (with rear door)	Maverick	M27 BM_STYLE
5. Station wagon	Vega	V27 VM_STYLE
6. Economy trunk		
7 Don't know		

```
                         Body Styles
                          Available
                       (see code above)

        Volkswagen          1, 3, 5
        Maverick            2
        Vega                1, 4, 5, 6
```

12. Which new small economy cars do you recall recently
     seeing advertised?

```
        The first car mentioned is          G17  F_FIRST
        The second car mentioned is         G18  F_SECOND
        The third car mentioned is          G19  F_THIRD
```

```
              Coding for Question 12

              Car              Code

              Pinto             1
              Vega              2
              Gremlin           3
              Maverick          4
              Volkswagen        5
              Toyota            6
              Duster            7
              Datsun            8
              Opel              9
```

13. Now, speaking only of the Maverick and Vega, in which
     media do you recall seeing these cars appear?

Media	Code (if mentioned)	Code (not mentioned)	Maverick	Vega
T.V.	2	0	G 20 FM_TV	G25 FV_TV
Radio	2	0	G 21 FM_RADIO	G26 FV_RADIO
Newspaper	2	0	G 22 FM_NEWS	G27 FV_NEWS
Magazines	2	0	G 23 FM_MAGZN	G28 FV_MAGZN
Billboards	2	0	G 24 FM_BILBD	G29 FV_BILBD

14. Do you recall viewing any portion of these special
    TV programs?

	Yes	No	
Changing Scene	( )	( )	G30 TV_CS
Golf Galaxie	( )	( )	G31 TV_GG
NCAA College Football	( )	( )	G32 TV_NCAA

15. During the last four weeks, how many Bonanza   G33 TV_BNZA
    programs have you viewed?

    Score   Score   Score
    0) None   2) 2 of the 4   4) 4 of the 4
    1) 1 of the 4   3) 3 of the 4

16. During the last four weeks, how many of the FBI   G34 TV_FBI
    programs have you viewed?

    Score   Score   Score
    0) None   2) 2 of the 4   4) 4 of the 4
    1) 1 of the 4   3) 3 of the 4

17. Now we want to get some information about your
    background. This information will help us to better
    understand the information you have given us about
    the Volkswagen, Pinto, and Vega.

17a. What is your sex?   Code   G35 SEX
                        Male   1
                      Female   2

17b. Into what category does your age fall?

Age	Code	Age	Code	G36 AGE
18-24	1	50-54	7	
25-29	2	55-59	8	
30-34	3	60-61+	9	
35-39	4			
40-44	5	Refused	0	
45-49	6			

17c. Into what range does your total 1969 income fall?
I do not need an exact figure.

		Use these categories if first set is not possible		
Try this scale first				
Income	Code	Income	Code	G37 INC
Under 5,000	1	Refused	0	
5,000-7,499	2	Under 10,000	2	
7,500-9,999	3	Over 10,000	5	
10,000-14,999	4			
15,000-19,999	5			
20,000+	6			

17d. Into which education category do you fall?

Finished	Code		G38 ED
6th grade	1		
8th grade	2		
12th grade	3		
some college	4		
all college	5		
some or all post-graduate study	6		
refused	0		

CENTRAL ASSET ACCOUNTS CASE

It was early 1985 and Jim Curtis had just left a meeting with his superior George Eberle, Executive Vice President of Shearson/Lehman's Consumer Markets Division. In the meeting, George had expressed his disappointment with the performance of Shearson's Financial Management Account (FMA). Jim had recently joined Shearson as Vice President of the Financial Product Group and his first assignment and prime responsibility was to improve the performance of the FMA by increasing the customer base and gaining market share.

George believed that the central asset account was the most important financial development in the last decade and the key product for building and maintaining a large retail market customer base. He was convinced that once a firm had sold a customer a central asset account, the customer would purchase the majority of his financial services and products from that company primarily based on convenience. In addition, he believed that there were high switching costs associated with the product for the following reasons:

- the amount of effort and inconvenience required by the customer to transfer his financial assets to another firm's central asset account;

This case was prepared by Professor John A. Howard and Chrisopher A. Green of Columbia University Graduate School of Business.

- the lack of product differentiation among the various central asset accounts in the market; and

- the customer's established personal relationships with the firm's broker or account executive.

The central asset account market was becoming crowded. Currently, there were 24 firms offering central asset accounts. In addition, it was a well-known fact that several large commercial banks and smaller brokerage firms were planning to offer central asset accounts. George believed that it was imperative for Shearson to have a well-developed and aggressive marketing strategy within 6 months or Shearson might risk losing its competitive position in the retail financial products market.

Jim had the responsibility of developing the strategy to reposition Shearson's Financial Management Account and his superior expected it within two months in order to have it reviewed by the Executive Committee of Shearson/Lehman/American Express.

Jim knew he did not have enough time to undertake an extensive nationwide market research project. Instead, he would have to use the results of a smaller survey conducted by his market research department to develop the strategy. The survey focused on the central asset accounts of four firms.

Merrill Lynch - Cash Management Account (CMA)

Shearson/Lehman/American Express - Financial Management

Account (FMA)

Dean Witter/Sears - Active Asset Account

Citibank - FOCUS Account

In addition, he has access to an analytic market research model called the Consumer Decision Model (CDM).

Your assignment is to assume the role of Jim Curtis and to undertake the following strategic project for Shearson's Financial Management Account.

1. Customer Analysis

    •   Develop a profile of the respondents surveyed in the study including key characteristics and demographics (e.g., sex, age, yearly income, etc.).

    •   Determine which product features of the central asset account are the most important to the respondents surveyed.

    •   Develop a profile of the "high potential customer" based on customers who have purchased or intend to purchase central asset accounts.

2. Competitive Analysis

    •   Develop for each of the four central asset account brands a Consumer Decision Model Diagram. Each Diagram should include a standardized coefficient (B-score) and significance measure (t-score) for each of the variable interrelationships in each model (e.g., $F \rightarrow B$, $F \rightarrow A$, $B \rightarrow A$. etc.).

175

- Assess the relative strength of each model and rank the models.

- Discuss the current competitive position of Shearson's FMA vis-a-vis the other three competitors (Merrill Lynch, Dean Witter, and Citibank).

3. Marketing Strategy

- Using the customer and competitive analyses, develop a marketing strategy and set of associated tactics to reposition Shearson's Financial Management Account. The structure, format and issues addressed in the strategy should follow those in Chapter 8. In addition, the following questions should be answered in the strategy:

  - What stage in the product life cycle is the central asset account?

  - How would you alter your strategy and tactics for the FMA in order to compete more effectively with commercial banks? Are there different factors to consider than when competing with brokerage firms?

  - You have a limited amount of dollars allocated for marketing. What is the most efficient way to spend your budget in order to maximize the number of accounts sold?

Be sure to include in your report on the case the following information to facilitate communicating your results.

1. Model specified in form of the CDM diagram with each construct defined and each relation shown by an arrow indicating the direction of causation.

2. Describe how each construct in the model is operationalized: which questions in the questionnaire were used to represent which variables and how each question was converted into the variable.

3. Diagram of model with respective regression coefficient shown in each relation, indicating whether the coefficient is the raw number or standardized, including the significance level of each coefficient in parentheses.

4. List of equations and showing the t-values for each question.

5. Discussion of your findings and their implications for practice at each of the major levels of management.

6. The order in which you deal with these topics is up to you. Some of the material may be put in appendices.

Notes on Central Asset Accounts

In 1977, Merrill Lynch commissioned the Stanford Research Institute to develop a list of new financial services that Merrill Lynch could provide to their customers. Stanford proposed a list of 50 ideas from which the Cash Management Account (CMA) was selected as an attractive opportunity for Merrill Lynch. Merrill Lynch began testing the CMA in a few markets during 1977 and one year later it was introduced nationally. The CMA has almost become the generic name for this type of product. By mid-1983, about 24 such accounts had been marketed, although it was four years before anyone followed Merrill Lynch into the market to provide a comparable service.

The central asset account is considered by many to be the single most important financial innovation of this decade. It attempts to meet an investor's full range of financial needs by providing maximum returns with minimum inconvenience for the investor. In order to purchase a central asset account, the investor is required to deposit and maintain in the account a minimum investment amount ($10,000-$20,000) in any combination of cash and gross market value of securities. In addition, the investor must pay an annual fee of $50-$100 and any appropriate fees for all brokerage and security transactions. The central asset account is an integrated financial service that incorporates three basic service components:

- Securities Account - conventional securities margin account

- Money Funds - a variety of short-term securities funds

  - Money funds -- money market securities (BAs, CDs, and Commericial Paper)

  - Government Securities Fund -- U.S. Government Securities (T-bills, T-notes, T-bonds, and agencies)

  - Tax Exempt Funds -- tax-exempt securities (municipal notes or bonds)

- Credit or Debit Card - Visa card issued by the affiliate bank of the brokerage house or AMEX card

The following is a more detailed description of each service:

- Securities Account - This is the primary component of the central asset account. It is a traditional margin account that the investor may use to borrow funds to either purchase or sell securities or options. The financial institution charges the investor interest for margin loans (securities not paid in full) that range from 3/4% to 2¼% above the rate charged by New York City banks to brokers to finance customer margin transactions.

- Money Funds - Any cash that may be transferred out of the securities account will then automatically be invested in shares of a Money Market Fund, Government Fund, or Tax Exempt Fund, depending on the investor preference. Dividends on money market shares are declared and reinvested on a daily basis. The money market funds are redeemed automatically if it is necessary to satisfy debit balances in the Securities Account or Credit Card Account.

- Credit Card Account - The affiliate bank will issue a credit card or debit card (usually a Visa or Amex) and checks to the central asset account customer. The authorization limit for purchases on the credit card is the sum of the uninvested free credit cash balances in securities plus the net asset value of money shares and the available margin loan of securities in the Securities Account. Since the balances in the accounts change daily, the investor's credit limit will vary.

In general, the central asset account provides six major services for investors:

1. The investor has convenient access to his assets through the use of a credit card or checking account.
2. Idle cash and dividends are swept daily into a high interest earning investment.
3. Investors have access to capital markets with the ability to charge security purchases to their accounts through the use of the margin account.
4. At the end of each month, the investor receives a consolidated statement with the transaction details of all his activities for the month.

5.   Since the investor can borrow up to the margin loan value of his securities portfolio, he has in effect immediate cash flow.

6.   The central asset account covers expenses automatically by taking money from the asset earning the lowest return.

Nearly all major securities firms and many banks offer a central asset account. While they have the same basic components, their features often differ. Among the features that distinguish accounts are:

- minimum initial investment required to open an account;

- yearly fee charged for the account;

- how frequent "sweeps" of free credit balances occur;

- whether a charge or debit card is issued for access (VISA or AMEX);

- whether the account is accessible through an ATM network; and

- the availability of a bank overdraft line of credit.

Questionnaire for Central Asset Account Industry

Graduate School of Business, Columbia University 1986

Number _____

1.* How much do you feel you know about the following
   Cash or Asset Management Accounts?

   a. Merrill Lynch's Cash Management Account

      Nothing at All 1 2 3 4 5 6 7 A Great Deal   V1 BM-KNO

   b. Dean Witter's Active Asset Account

      Nothing at All 1 2 3 4 5 6 7 A Great Deal   V1 BD-KNO

   c. Shearson's Financial Management Account

      Nothing at All 1 2 3 4 5 6 7 A Great Deal   V1 BS-KNO

   d. Citibank's Focus Account

      Nothing at All 1 2 3 4 5 6 7 A Great Deal   V1 BG-KNO

---

*Questions 11 through 22 originally appeared at the beginning of the
 questionnaire but to facilitate the analysis of the data, they have
 been moved to the later position.

DO NOT COMPLETE FOR CODING USE ONLY

(Record number of points mentioned for:)

Merrill Lynch	_____	V2 FM-REC
Dean Witter	_____	V2 FD-REC
Shearson	_____	V2 FS-REC
Citibank	_____	V2 FG-REC

2. What do you recall from the advertising of each of the following firms?

Merrill Lynch _____

_____

Dean Witter _____

_____

Shearson _____

_____

Citibank _____

_____

3. What thoughts came to mind when you saw the advertisements for:

Merrill Lynch's CMA _____   V3 FM-TH

_____

Dean Witter's Active Asset Account _____   V3 FD-TH

_____

Shearson's Financial Management Account _____   V3 FS-TH

_____

Citibank's Focus Account _____   V3 FC-TH

_____

4. When you think of (Company Name) or the (Company Product, e.g., CMA) is there any trademark, symbol, or other identifying mark you can recall?

Merrill Lynch   1) Yes   0) No

If so, what is the trademark? _____   V4 BM-TR

Dean Witter   1) Yes   0) No

If so, what is the trademark? _____   V4 BD-TR

Shearson   1) Yes   0) No

If so, what is the trademark? _____   V4 BS-TR

Citibank   1) Yes   0) No

If so, what is the trademark? _____   V4 BC-TR

5. When you think of (Company Name) is there any slogan
    or phrase you can recall?

    Merrill Lynch   1) Yes   0) No

    If so, what is the slogan? _____   V5 BM-SLO

    Dean Witter   1) Yes   0) No

    If so, what is the slogan? _____   V5 BD-SLO

Shearson   1) Yes   0) No

    If so, what is the slogan? _____   V5 BS-SLO

Citibank   1) Yes   0) No

    If so, what is the slogan? _____   V5 BC-SLO

6. Now I will read a list of ways you might have heard of
    or seen Cash/Asset Management Accounts advertised.
    After I read each type of source, please tell me
    whether you have seen or heard about the Cash/Asset
    Management account this way very often, sometimes,
    rarely, or never.

Merrill Lynch CMA

Media Source	Never	Rarely	Sometimes	Often	Very Often		
T.V.	1	2	3	4	5	V6	FM-TV
Radio	1	2	3	4	5	V7	FM-RAD
Newspaper	1	2	3	4	5	V8	FM-NEW
Investment Newsletter	1	2	3	4	5	V9	FM-INV
Business Magazines	1	2	3	4	5	V10	FM-BMAG
Other Magazines	1	2	3	4	4	V11	FM-OMAG

Dean Witter Active Asset Account

Media Source	Never	Rarely	Sometimes	Often	Very Often		
T.V.	1	2	3	4	5	V6	FD-TV
Radio	1	2	3	4	5	V7	FD-RAD
Newspaper	1	2	3	4	5	V8	FD-NEW
Investment Newsletter	1	2	3	4	5	V9	FD-INV
Business Magazines	1	2	3	4	5	V10	FD-BMAG
Other Magazines	1	2	3	4	4	V11	FD-OMAG

Shearson Financial Management Account

Media Source	Never	Rarely	Sometimes	Often	Very Often		
T.V.	1	2	3	4	5	V6	FS-TV
Radio	1	2	3	4	5	V7	FS-RAD
Newspaper	1	2	3	4	5	V8	FS-NEW
Investment Newsletter	1	2	3	4	5	V9	FS-INV
Business Magazines	1	2	3	4	5	V10	FS-BMAG
Other Magazines	1	2	3	4	4	V11	FS-OMAG

Citibank Focus Account

Media Source	Never	Rarely	Sometimes	Often	Very Often		
T.V.	1	2	3	4	5	V6	FC-TV
Radio	1	2	3	4	5	V7	FC-RAD
Newspaper	1	2	3	4	5	V8	FC-NEW
Investment Newsletter	1	2	3	4	5	V9	FC-INV
Business Magazines	1	2	3	4	5	V10	FC-BMAG
Other Magazines	1	2	3	4	4	V11	FC-OMAG

7. How likely are you in the next six months to invest in the following:

Merrill Lynch CMA

Definitely Don't Intend	1 2 3 4 5 6 7	Definitely Intend	V12 IM

Dean Witter Active

Definitely Don't Intend	1 2 3 4 5 6 7	Definitely Intend	V12 ID

Shearson Financial Management Account

Definitely Don't Intend	1 2 3 4 5 6 7	Definitely Intend	V12 IS

Citibank Focus Account

    Definitely   1 2 3 4 5 6 7   Definitely V12 IC
    Don't Intend   Intend

8. How confident are you in your ability to judge the quality of:

Merrill Lynch Cash Management Account

    Not at All   1 2 3 4 5 6 7   Very   V13 CM
    Confident   Confident

Dean Witter Active Asset Account

    Not at All   1 2 3 4 5 6 7   Very   V13 CD
    Confident   Confident

Shearson Financial Management Account

    Not at All   1 2 3 4 5 6 7   Very   V13 CS
    Confident   Confident

Citibank Focus Account

    Not at All   1 2 3 4 5 6 7   Very   V13 CC
    Confident   Confident

9a. How much do you agree or disagree with the following statements about the various accounts?

                        Disagree   Agree

Merrill Lynch CMA

    Is Convenient   1 2 3 4 5 6 7   V14 AM-CONV

Dean Witter Active Asset Account

    Is Convenient   1 2 3 4 5 6 7   V14 AD-CONV

Shearson Financial Management Account

    Is Convenient   1 2 3 4 5 6 7   V14 AS-CONV

Citibank Focus Account

    Is Convenient   1 2 3 4 5 6 7   V14 AC-CONV

9b. How much do you agree or disagree with the following
    statements about the various accounts?

                   <u>Disagree</u>   <u>Agree</u>

<u>Merrill Lynch CMA</u>

    Extensive Credit   1   2   3   4   5   6   7   V15 AM-CR
    Line

<u>Dean Witter Active Asset Account</u>

    Extensive Credit   1   2   3   4   5   6   7   V15 AD-CR
    Line

<u>Shearson Financial Management Account</u>

    Extensive Credit   1   2   3   4   5   6   7   V15 AS-CR
    Line

<u>Citibank Focus Account</u>

    Extensive Credit   1   2   3   4   5   6   7   V15 AC-CR
    Line

9c. How much do you agree or disagree with the following
    statements about the various accounts?

                   <u>Disagree</u>   <u>Agree</u>

<u>Merrill Lynch CMA</u>

    High Return Rate   1   2   3   4   5   6   7   V16 AM-RET

<u>Dean Witter Active Asset Account</u>

    High Return Rate   1   2   3   4   5   6   7   V16 AD-RET

<u>Shearson Financial Management Account</u>

    High Return Rate   1   2   3   4   5   6   7   V16 AS-RET

<u>Citibank Focus Account</u>

    High Return Rate   1   2   3   4   5   6   7   V16 AC-RET

9d. How much do you agree or disagree with the following
    statements about the various accounts?

Merrill Lynch CMA

    Timely Investment 1 2 3 4 5 6 7   V17 AM-SWP
    of Idle Cash
    (Cash Sweep)

Dean Witter Active Asset Account

    Timely Investment 1 2 3 4 5 6 7   V17 AD-SWP
    of Idle Cash
    (Cash Sweep)

Shearson Financial Management Account

    Timely Investment 1 2 3 4 5 6 7   V17 AS-SWP
    of Idle Cash
    (Cash Sweep)

Citibank Focus Account

    Timely Investment 1 2 3 4 5 6 7   V17 AC-SWP
    of Idle Cash
    (Cash Sweep)

9e. How much do you agree or disagree with the following
    statements about the various accounts?

                  Disagree   Agree

Merrill Lynch CMA

    A Comprehensive 1 2 3 4 5 6 7   V18 AM-TRAN
    Transaction
    Statement

Dean Witter Active Asset Account

    A Comprehensive 1 2 3 4 5 6 7   V18 AD-TRAN
    Transaction
    Statement

Shearson Financial Management Account

    A Comprehensive 1 2 3 4 5 6 7   V18 AS-TRAN
    Transaction
    Statement

Citibank Focus Account

A Comprehensive	1	2	3	4	5	6	7		V18	AC-TRAN
Transaction										
Statement										

9f. How much do you agree or disagree with the following
statements about the various accounts?

                 Disagree   Agree

Merrill Lynch CMA

Annual fee is	1	2	3	4	5	6	7		V19	AM-FEE
Reasonable										

Dean Witter Active Asset Account

Annual fee is	1	2	3	4	5	6	7		V19	AD-FEE
Reasonable										

Shearson Financial Management Account

Annual fee is	1	2	3	4	5	6	7		V19	AS-FEE
Reasonable										

Citibank Focus Account

Annual fee is	1	2	3	4	5	6	7		V19	AC-FEE
Reasonable										

9g. How much do you agree or disagree with the following
statements about the various accounts?

                 Disagree   Agree

Merrill Lynch CMA

Minimum Investment	1	2	3	4	5	6	7		V20	AM-MIN
Level is Reasonable										

Dean Witter Active Asset Account

Minimum Investment	1	2	3	4	5	6	7		V20	AD-MIN
Level is Reasonable										

Shearson Financial Management Account

    Minimum Investment 1   2   3   4   5   6   7   V20 AS-MIN
    Level is Reasonable

Citibank Focus Account

    Minimum Investment 1   2   3   4   5   6   7   V20 AC-MIN
    Level is Reasonable

9h. How much do you agree or disagree with the following
statements about the various accounts?

                    Disagree   Agree

Merrill Lynch CMA

    Good Reputation   1   2   3   4   5   6   7   V21 AM-REP
    of Brokerage House

Dean Witter Active Asset Account

    Good Reputation   1   2   3   4   5   6   7   V21 AD-REP
    of Brokerage House

Shearson Financial Management Account

    Good Reputation   1   2   3   4   5   6   7   V21 AS-REP
    of Brokerage House

Citibank Focus Account

    Good Reputation   1   2   3   4   5   6   7   V21 AC-REP
    of Brokerage House

9i. How much do you agree or disagree with the following
statements about the various accounts?

                    Disagree   Agree

Merrill Lynch CMA

    High Confidence   1   2   3   4   5   6   7   V22 AM-CONF
    in Broker's
    Recommendation

	Disagree						Agree			

Disagree   Agree

Dean Witter Active Asset Account

    High Confidence   1   2   3   4   5   6   7   V22 AD-CONF
    in Broker's
    Recommendation

Shearson Financial Management Account

    High Confidence   1   2   3   4   5   6   7   V22 AS-CONF
    in Broker's
    Recommendation

Citibank Focus Account

    High Confidence   1   2   3   4   5   6   7   V22 AC-CONF
    in Broker's
    Recommendation

9j. How much do you agree or disagree with the following statements about the various accounts?

Disagree   Agree

Merrill Lynch CMA

    High Level of   1   2   3   4   5   6   7   V23 AM-SERV
    Personal Service

Dean Witter Active Asset Account

    High Level of   1   2   3   4   5   6   7   V23 AD-SERV
    Personal Service

Shearson Financial Management Account

    High Level of   1   2   3   4   5   6   7   V23 AS-SERV
    Personal Service

Citibank Focus Account

    High Level of   1   2   3   4   5   6   7   V23 AC-SERV
    Personal Service

9k. How much do you like the company's Cash/Asset Management Account?

191

	Not at All						Very Much	

Merrill Lynch CMA

| | 1 | 2 | 3 | 4 | 5 | 6 | 7 | V24 AG-M |

Dean Witter Active Asset Account

| | 1 | 2 | 3 | 4 | 5 | 6 | 7 | V24 AG-D |

Shearson Financial Management Account

| | 1 | 2 | 3 | 4 | 5 | 6 | 7 | V24 AG-S |

Citibank Focus Account

| | 1 | 2 | 3 | 4 | 5 | 6 | 7 | V24 AG-C |

10. How important are the following Cash/Asset Management Account criteria to you?

	Unimportant				Important			
a. Ease of use	1	2	3	4	5	6	7	V25 W-CONV
b. Level of Credit Line	1	2	3	4	5	6	7	V26 W-CR
c. Return rate (yield) on Cash/Asset Management Account Money Market Fund	1	2	3	4	5	6	7	V27 W-RET
d. Time Investment of Idle Cash (Cash Sweep)	1	2	3	4	5	6	7	V28 W-SWP
e. Comprehensiveness of Transaction Statement	1	2	3	4	5	6	7	V29 W-TRAN
f. Size of Annual Fee	1	2	3	4	5	6	7	V30 W-FEE
g. Minimum required Investment Level of Cash/Asset Management Account	1	2	3	4	5	6	7	V31 W-MIN
h. Reputation of Brokerage House	1	2	3	4	5	6	7	V32 W-REP

i. Confidence in   1   2   3   4   5   6   7   V33 W-CONF
   Broker's Recommenda-
   tions

j. Quality of Personal   1   2   3   4   5   6   7   V34 W-SERV
   Service

11.   Do you know what a Cash/Asset Management Account is?
      Examples include Merrill Lynch's Cash Management
      Account (CMA), Dean Witter's Active Asset Account,
      Shearson's Financial Management Account, or Citibank's
      Personal Asset Account (Focus).

                  1) Yes   0) No   V35 F-CAM

      If you answer "No" to question 1, go to question 3.

12.   Do you presently have a Cash/Asset Management Account?

                  1) Yes   0) No   V36 P-CAM

      If no, then skip 2a and 2b.

      If yes, which company? _____

12a. How satisifed are you with it?

                  1) Extremely dissatisfied   V37 S-CAM
                  2) Dissatisfied
                  3) Indifferent
                  4) Satisfied
                  5) Extremely Satisfied

12b. How long have you had your Cash/Asset Management
      Account?

                  1) one month   V38 OWN-CAM
                  2) six months
                  3) one year
                  4) two years
                  5) more than two years

13. If you do not now have one, what are the chances of your opening a Cash/Asset Management Account in the next six months?

1) Definitely Not   V39 I-CAM
2) Probably Not
3) Probably
4) Definitely

14. Do you presently invest part of your income and savings?

1) Yes   0) No   V40 INV

If yes, do you invest in:

Stocks	1) Yes	0) No	V41 P-STOC
Corporate Bonds	1) Yes	0) No	V42 P-CBON
Government Securities	1) Yes	0) No	V43 P-GOVT
Tax-Exempt Bonds	1) Yes	0) No	V44 P-TE
Mutual Funds	1) Yes	0) No	V45 P-MUT
Real Estate	1) Yes	0) No	V46 P-RE
Savings Account	1) Yes	0) No	V47 P-SAV
Other	1) Yes	0) No	V48 P-OTH

15. How often do you make an investment decision regarding your investment portfolio? (An investment decision is a decision to buy or sell any financial instrument such as stocks or bonds.)

Not Very Often   Very Often   V49 INV-FREQ

1   2   3   4   5   6   7   8   9

Use the following scale:

Daily	= 9
2-3 Times a Week	= 7 or 8
Weekly	= 6
Bi-Weekly	= 5
Monthly	= 4
Every 3 Months	= 3
Every 6 Months	= 2
Once a Year or Less	= 1

16. How well informed do you consider yourself in the stock market and its daily events?

        Not Very   1 2 3 4 5 6 7 Very Well   V50 INF-SM
        Well Informed   Informed

17. Do you presently have a stockbroker or money manager?

              1) Yes   0) No   V51 MON-MAR

     If Yes, then which brokerage house or
     company? _____

18. How frequently do you discuss your stock portfolio and
     investment decisions with your broker?

        Never   1 2 3 4 5 6 7   Very Often   V52 DS-FREQ

19. Do you buy stocks on margin?

              1) Yes   0) No   V53 P-MARG

20. Do you consider yourself a conservative, risky-
     speculative, or somewhere in between?

        Risky   1 2 3 4 5 6 7 Conservative V54 RISK

21. Are you employed in any area of the financial services
     (investment banking, commercial banking, etc.)?

              1) Yes   0) No   V55 FINSER

22. How much of a difference is there between the Cash/
     Asset Management Accounts offered by the leading
     financial institutions?

        Very Great   1 2 3 4 5 6 7   Not at All V56 CAMDIF

23. Indicate the following people with whom you have discussed Cash/Asset Management Accounts.

Spouse	1) Yes	0) No	V57	F-SP
Relative	1) Yes	0) No	V58	F-REL
Account Executive	1) Yes	0) No	V59	F-ACEX
Business Colleague	1) Yes	0) No	V60	F-BC
Friend	1) Yes	0) No	V61	F-FR

24. In which of the following media do you recall seeing Cash/Asset Management Accounts advertised?

Media

T.V.	1) Yes	0) No	V62	F-TV
Radio	1) Yes	0) No	V63	F-RAD
Newspaper	1) Yes	0) No	V64	F-NEWS
Investment Lit./				
Newsletter	1) Yes	0) No	V65	F-INL
Business Magazines	1) Yes	0) No	V66	F-BMAG
Other Magazines	1) Yes	0) No	V67	F-OMAG

25. What is your sex?

	Code	V68 SEX
Male	1	
Female	2	

26. Into what category does your age fall?

Age	Code	V69 AGE
18-25	1	
26-30	2	
31-35	3	
36-40	4	
41-50	5	
51-60	6	
60 or over	7	
Refused	8	

27. I will read a list of income ranges. Please tell me
    into which range your family income for 1984 falls.
    I do not need an exact figure.

Income	Code
Under $20,000	1
$20,001-$40,000	2
$40,001-$60,000	3
$60,001-$100,000	4
$100,001-$150,000	5
$150,001-$200,000	6
over $200,000	7

V70 INC

28. What is the approximate size of your investment
    portfolio?

	Code
$0-$10,000	1
$10,001-$20,000	2
$20,001-$30,000	3
$40,001-$50,000	5
$50,001-$60,000	6
$60,001-$70,000	7
$70,001-$80,000	8
$80,001-$90,000	9
$90,001-$100,000	10
$100,001 or over	11

V71 INVP

29. What is your highest level of education?

Completed	Code
6th grade	1
8th grade	2
High School	3
Some College	4
4-year College	5
Some Graduate	6
Post-Graduate Degree	7

V72 ED

30. Are you married? If so, are you or your spouse
    retired?

	Code	V73 MARR
Husband	1	V74 SPRET
Spouse	2	
Both	3	
Neither	4	

31. Is your family a two-income family? In other words,
    are both you and your spouse employed?

    1) Yes   0) No   V75 IIFINC

32. If yes, what is your occupation?

	Code	V76 OCC
Professional		
(Lawyer, Doctor)	1	
Executive		
(Upper Management)	2	
Managerial		
(Middle Management)	3	
Professor/Teacher	4	
Sales	5	
Clerical	6	
Craftsman		
(Electrician)	7	
Blue Collar	8	
Student	9	
Unemployed	10	
Other	11	_____

33. What is your spouse's occupation?

	Code	V77 SPOCC
Professional		
(Lawyer, Doctor)	1	
Executive		
(Upper Management)	2	
Managerial		
(Middle Management)	3	
Professor/Teacher	4	
Sales	5	
Clerical	6	

Crafstman	
(Electrician)	7
Blue Collar	8
Student	9
Unemployed	10
Other	11 _____

34. In what industry are you employed?

Code   V78 INDOCC

Financial Services	1
Legal Services	2
Medical Services	3
Manufacturing Industry	4
Service Industry	5
Education	6
High Tech. (computers)	7
Other	8 _____

35. In what industry is your spouse employed?

Code   V79 SPINC

Financial Services	1
Legal Services	2
Medical Services	3
Manufacturing Industry	4
Service Industry	5
Education	6
High Tech. (computers)	7
Other	8 _____

36. Do you do most of the investing for your family or does someone else? If someone else, please specify who.

Code   V80 INVEST

Self	1
Spouse	2 Husband or Wife
Relative	3
Friend	4
Financial Advisor	
(e.g., stockbroker)	5

ALPHA OIL: DECEPTIVE AND CORRECTIVE ADVERTISING*

In the mid-60's, Ralph Nader attacked the Federal Trade Commission
for failing to provide adequate protection for the consumer. This
stimulus led to the appointment of an American Bar Association Committee to investigate the Commission. Miles Kilpatrick was the Chairman
of the Committee and Robert Pitofsky was the Executive Director. Not
long after the Committee rendered its highly critical report, Mr.
Kilpatrick was asked to be the Chairman of the Commission. He accepted
and brought in Pitofsky as director of the newly formed FTC's Bureau of
Consumer Protection. One of the existing Commissioners, Mary Gardiner
Jones, was already quite critical of the Commission's performance on
the consumer side. A number of innovations in regulating advertising
were soon introduced.

The original FTC Act (1914) provided for regulating deceptive
advertising, but the purpose -- at least as it came to be interpreted
-- was to protect "competition." Not until 1938 was the Act amended to
direct the Commission specifically to protect the consumer from deceptive practices. The amendment went further, however, and stated
"deceptive and unfair" practices. So far, most of the regulation has
come under the deception rubric and the unfairness side has not been
exploited by the Commission. It opens up a large future potential of
FTC action, however.

---

*By John A. Howard and Donald H. Lehmann, School of Business, Columbia
University, 1974.

One of the innovations initiated during Mr. Kilpatrick's tenure was corrective advertising. It was felt at the Commission that the traditional cease-and-desist orders for violation of deceptive advertising were mere slaps on the wrist of the offender and provided no real deterrent to future violations. Corrective advertising, it was thought, would offer a much greater deterrent. The offending company would be directed to run some portion of its advertising for a period of time, perhaps a year, in which it said that its previous ad was not true. The Alpha Oil case was initiated in this environment of changing FTC policy.

The Alpha Oil Company,* which both refines crude and sells gas at retail, was charged by the Federal Trade Commission in 1972 with running deceptive advertising. In its complaint -- a document formally setting forth the charge -- the FTC cited the following two ads as being characterized by deception.

> PARAGRAPH TEN: Typical of the statements and representations made and demonstrations used by respondents in their advertising of Alphane gasoline, but not limited thereto, are the following television commercials:
>
> A.   In "Trains," an automobile of unstated make, model, and performance specifications is supplied with Alphane gasoline of unstated octane rating. The automobile is then coupled with three empty railroad cars, two boxcars and a caboose, standing stationary on a siding. The automobile, after a signal from the announcer, proceeds to pull away with the load of approximately 100 tons.
>
> ANNOUNCER: We're . . . demonstrating an "unusual" gasoline. A gasoline that will help this car's engine put out every last ounce of power it has.

---

*This name is fictitious, but the details are true.

What makes this gasoline unusual? It's blended with the
action of Alphane 260 . . . the highest octane gasoline at
any station, anywhere.

There you have it. Alphane 260 Action in this car is pulling
over 100 tons. Not just one boxcar but two boxcars and a
caboose. This is the same 260 Action you get in every
Alphane blend.

Because Alphane's Custom Blending Pump blends just
the right amount of 260 . . . into every gallon of premium,
middle premiums, even regular.

You're seeing Alphane premium deliver in this car. [Repeat
of demonstration.] Let Alphane, with 260 Action, deliver in
your car.

Get Alphane 260 Action. Action to be used. Not abused.

B.   In "Coliseum," the message is essentially the same. An
automobile of unstated make, model, and performance specifications
is supplied with Alphane gasoline of unstated octane rating. The
automobile then proceeds, on cue, to pull an empty U-haul trailer
of unstated weight up a ramp specially constructed over a bank of
seats in the Los Angeles Coliseum.

ANNOUNCER: We're going to drive a car, pulling this trailer from
      the field to . . . the top of the stands to demonstrate an
      unusual gasoline. A gasoline that will help this car's
      engine put out every bit of power it has.

What makes this gasoline unusual? It's blended with the
action of Alphane 260 . . . the highest octane gasoline at
any station, anywhere.

With 260 action, the car and trailer go up the ramp just like
that.

You get the same 260 Action at Alphane . . .

Watch again as Alphane regular . . . delivers in this car.
[Repeat of demonstration.]

Let Alphane, with 260 Action, deliver in your car.

Get Alphane 260 Action. Action to be used. Not abused.

PARAGRAPH ELEVEN: By and through the use of the aforesaid
statements, representations, and demonstrations, and others
similar thereto not specifically set out herein, respondents have

represented and are now representing directly, and by implication that:

A.   Blending Alphane's highest octane gasoline, "260," into Alphane's lower octane gasolines results in blends of gasoline that by reason of their respective octane levels provide more engine power than do competing gasolines having octane ratings comparable to Alphane's blends.

B.   Blending Alphane's highest octane gasoline, "260," into Alphane's lower octane gasolines conveys to resulting blends of Alphane gasoline the octane benefits of Alphane "260," or "260 Action."

C.   Only when operated on the octane of Alphane's "Custom Blended" gasolines will automobile engines operate at maximum power and performance.

D.   Said demonstrations are evidence which actually prove that Alphane gasolines blended with "Alphane 260 Action" are unique or unusual in that they alone provide the power necessary to enable an automobile to perform the task depicted.

PARAGRAPH TWELVE: In truth and fact:

A.   Alphane's gasoline blends do not provide more engine power by reason of their respective octane levels than do competing gasolines of comparable octane rating.

B.   Blending Alphane "260" into Alphane's lower octane gasolines conveys to resulting blends of Alphane gasoline no more octane benefits than provided by the octane level of the resultant blends.

C.   Octane is a measure of motor fuel antiknock quality, and to the extent that octane relates to power and performance any gasoline of sufficient octane will provide maximum power and performance.

D.   Said demonstrations are not evidence which actually prove that Alphane gasolines blended with "Alphane 260 Action" are unique or unusual. Other gasolines of comparable octane rating will also provide the power necessary to enable an automobile to perform the tasks depicted.

Therefore, the aforesaid statements and representations, and demonstrations used in conjunction therewith, as set forth in Paragraphs Ten and Eleven were, and are, false, misleading, and deceptive.

203

PARAGRAPH THIRTEEN: The aforesaid advertisements and demonstrations, and others similar but not specifically set out herein, have falsely represented, and are now falsely representing directly and by implication, that Alphane gasoline has unique qualities not found in other brands of gasoline. With respect to octane, all automobile gasolines, regardless of brand name, will provide maximum power and performance in an automobile engine if sufficient gasoline octane is provided. The aforesaid acts and practices were, and are now, false, misleading, deceptive and unfair, and therefore constitute unfair methods of competition in commerce.

As a result of reviewing these ads, the FTC came to the following official conclusion:

PARAGRAPH FOURTEEN: The use by respondents of the aforesaid false, misleading, and deceptive statements, representations and demonstrations, including the misleading and deceptive statements and representations made in connection with said demonstrations, has had, and now has, the tendency and capacity to mislead and deceive a substantial portion of the purchasing public into erroneous and mistaken belief that said statements and representations were and are true, and into the purchasing of a substantial quantity of respondent Alpha Oil Company's gasoline because of such erroneous and mistaken belief.

PARAGRAPH FIFTEEN: The aforesaid acts and practices of respondents, as herein alleged, were and are all to the prejudice and injury of the public and of respondents' competitors, and constituted, and now constitute, unfair and deceptive acts and practices in commerce and unfair methods of competition in commerce in violation of Section 5 of the Federal Trade Commission Act.

In terms of the usual practice, a hearing was set, before a hearing examiner (Administrative Law Judge), at which the FTC lawyer would state the Commission's case and the Alpha Oil Company could "appear and show cause why an order should not be entered requiring (it) to cease and desist from the violations of law charged in this complaint." Alpha Oil could thus appear and defend itself, or it could

file an admission that the allegations were true and then discontinue
running the ads.

In this case, however, the Commission went a step further and
attached a more serious penalty than merely cease and desist. It
ordered corrective advertising.

> IT IS FURTHER ORDERED that respondent Alpha Oil Company do
> forthwith cease and desist from publishing or causing to be
> published, or broadcasting or causing to be broadcast, any adver-
> tisement for Alphane gasoline for a period of one year from the
> date that this order becomes final unless it is clearly and
> conspicuously disclosed in any such advertisement that, contrary
> to prior representations found in that company's advertising for
> Alphane gasoline, to the extent that automobile performance
> depends on octane levels, automobiles do not perform better with
> Alphane than with other gasolines of equal octane. Said disclo-
> sure must consist of not less than twenty-five percent of the
> total space used for each advertisement in printed form and not
> less than twenty-five percent of the total time devoted to each
> advertisement disseminated on radio or television.

This latter penalty, if accepted, might be damaging for the Company's
customer relations. Consequently, the Company viewed the two actions
quite separately. The admission of deception and acceptance of the
cease and desist order was one thing. Accepting the corrective remedy,
however, was quite another.

The procedure is for the Administrative Law Judge, based on the
hearing, to make a recommendation for disposing of the case, which is
then passed upon by the Commission as a whole. Consequently, the FTC
is sometimes charged with being investigator, judge, and jury all
combined.

The Company did appear at the hearing before the Administrative
Law Judge to "show cause why an order should not be entered requiring

you to cease and desist from the violations of law charged in this complaint." At the hearing, the Commission's attorney presented its case and in so doing had as an expert witness Professor Smith (a fictitious name), a distinguished marketing professor from a leading university. In his testimony, he drew upon market research data that the Commission had subpoenaed from the Alpha Oil Company. These data are shown in Tables 2 and 3, attached. He first testified as to the quality of these data and concluded with "the sample design and interviewing procedures could have been improved upon, but I think it is adequate."

The most important substantive questions had to do with the effect of advertising. Did it increase the consumer's attitude toward Alphane and increase his purchases? Table 4 was intended to throw some light on this issue. Also, did the effect carry over to a point where corrective advertising would be justified? Table 5 is relevant here. Professor Smith's position on attitudes was unequivocal:

> Once consumers have a familiarity with an object or brand, once they are aware of it, once they have tried it, used it, purchased it, seen the advertising, their attitudes become relatively fixed and it is very difficult to change those attitudes.
>
> . . . therefore, if you only had the market share information to look at you would probably conclude that the advertising did not affect the market share. But I ask myself this question: Is it reasonable to believe that the behavior of no one was influenced by this advertising? And my answer is, no, it is not reasonable to believe that. So I wouldn't want to make strong assertions that this advertising did have an effect -- certainly, it did not have a pronounced effect on consumer behavior, or consumer choice. But I do not believe that it is reasonable to believe that no consumer was influenced.

FTC attorney: Dr. Smith, is it reasonable to infer that gasoline sales of Alpha Oil Company are greater than they would have been if the two advertising themes had not been employed and the attitudes had not been favorably affected?

Dr. Smith: Yes, it is reasonable to believe that. It is unreasonable not to believe it; I would prefer to state it that way.

What would you do in this situation had you been the president of Alpha Oil Company? What would have been your recommendations to your board of directors? Would you have accepted both charges: deception and corrective advertising? Would you have accepted neither, or would you have accepted one but not the other? Be as explicit as you can in supporting your position and use the attached data as fully as you can.

TABLE 1

Breakdown of Fall 1971 Results by User Category

Percent Who Identified Current Claim

Brand	Steady Users of Brand	Occasional Users of Brand	Non-Users of Brand	Total
ALPHANE	60%	51%	37%	40%
Comp. Avg.	42%	39%	28%	31%
Amoco	41%	60%	48%	49%
Arco	39%	31%	17%	21%
B.P.	35%	31%	12%	14%
Esso	23%	20%	15%	17%
Gulf	42%	44%	30%	33%
Mobil	63%	51%	35%	40%
Shell	54%	53%	37%	42%
Sohio	22%	14%	16%	17%
Standard	57%	56%	48%	52%
Texaco	41%	25%	19%	21%

Comments:

Awareness of the Alphane advertising claim is at about the same level
as last year. Standard, Amoco, and Shell claims all have somewhat
higher identification than the Alphane claim.

TABLE 2

Respondents' Usage of Alphane and 9 or 10 Other Brands
Percent of <u>respondents in mkts.</u> where brand sold who:

Said bought brand in "Past 3 Months or So"
(shown in Spring '68)

	S 66	F 66	S 67	F 67	S 68	F 68	S 69	F 69	S 70	F 70	F 71	F 72	S 66 to F 72
Alpha	29½	28	26½	30	25	27	26½	24½	24½	24½	19	19	-10
Amoco	22	22	21	22	21	19½	20½	19½	19½	18½	17	17	- 5
Arco	20	24	19½	22½	18	23½	19½	20	19	18	12	17	- 3
BP	--	--	--	--	--	--	--	--	--	8	9	--	--
Esso	47	48½	46	45	43½	43	41	40	42	26	34	34	-13
Gulf	20½	23½	21	21½	19½	23	20	24	21½	17½	16½	17	- 3
Mobil	17	19½	16	21	16	21	18½	22½	22½	19	16	19	+ 2
Shell	30	29	29	29½	29½	32	32	33	33½	27½	30	36	+ 6
Sohio	72½	65	69	69½	67½	64	64	60	64	58	49	55½	-17
Standard	60	61½	63½	62	56	56½	56½	56	60	49½	50½	50	-10
Texaco	17	21½	20½	19½	17	20	17½	17½	15½	16	16	15	- 2

From Spring '66 through Fall '68, Alpha was down only 2½%; but from Fall '68 thgrough Fall '72, Alpha was down sharply.

TABLE 3

Usage

Percent of respondents who said they "Usually Buy" brand
(In mkts. where brand sold)

	S 66	F 66	S 67	F 67	S 68	F 68	S 69	F 69	S 70	F 70	F 71	F 72	S 66 to F 72
Alpha	13	11	10½	11½	10	12	11	10½	10½	10½	8	8	- 5
Amoco	9	10½	7½	8½	9	8½	9	9	9	8½	8	8	- 1
Arco	7	8	7	8	6	8½	7½	10½	7	8	4½	8	+ 1
BP	--	--	--	--	--	--	--	--	--	3½	3	--	--
Esso	21½	20½	21½	19½	19	20	17	17	20	12	16	16	- 5½
Gulf	7	6	6½	5½	5	7	5½	8½	6½	6	6	5½	- 1½
Mobil	7	7½	6	7	6½	8	8½	9	10	7½	5½	7	0
Shell	10½	10½	11	11	11½	12	2	13	13½	10½	13½	15	+ 4½
Sohio	38	31½	33½	38½	34	33	35½	30	33½	30	26	26	-12
Standard	26	27	33½	29½	23	26	23	26½	26	26	26½	20	- 6
Texaco	5	7	6½	5	5	5½	5½	6	5	5½	6	4½	- ½

Alphane dropped 4th from highest in '66-'72, but 3rd from highest Fall '68-Fall '72.

TABLE 4

Rating on Eight Factors by User Type

(Fall, 1970)

Factor	Brand	Steady Users of Brand	Occasional Users of Brand	Non-Users of Brand	Total
Good for	Alphane	3.5	2.0	0.9	1.3
Your Engine	Competitive Avg.	3.3	1.9	1.2	1.6
Helps Reduce	Alphane	0.4	-0.2	-0.2	-0.1
Air Polution	Competitive Avg.	0.7	0.1	0.3	0.3
Good Mileage	Alphane	3.1	1.9	0.8	1.2
Per Gallon	Competitive Avg.	2.9	1.6	0.9	1.3
Many Stations	Alphane	3.3	2.1	1.3	1.6
Available	Competitive Avg.	3.4	2.6	1.7	2.0
Reasonably Priced Major Brand	Alphane	2.8	1.6	1.0	1.2
	Competitive Avg.	2.7	1.4	0.9	1.2
Provides Plenty	Alphane	3.9	2.4	1.2	1.6
of Power	Competitive Avg.	3.1	2.1	1.1	1.5
Clean, Attractive Locations	Alphane	3.7	2.1	1.6	1.9
	Competitive Avg.	3.5	2.4	1.7	2.1
Prompt, Courteous Service	Alphane	3.8	2.5	1.3	1.7
	Competitive Avg.	3.3	2.5	1.5	1.9

TABLE 5

Rating on Eight Factors by User Type

Fall, 1972

Gasoline Characteristics	Importance Rating	Brand	Steady Users of Brand	Occassional Users of Brand	Non-Users of Brand	Total
Good Mileage Per Gallon	3.5	Alphane	3.3	2.2	1.3	1.6
		Comp. Avg.	3.2	2.2	1.3	1.7
Provides Quick Starts	3.0	Alphane	3.6	2.3	1.4	1.7
		Comp. Avg.	3.1	2.1	1.3	1.7
Cleans Your Engine	2.6	Alphane	2.4	1.7	0.9	1.1
		Comp. Avg.	2.6	1.6	1.0	1.3
Low Price	2.2	Alphane	1.8	1.0	0.7	0.9
		Comp. Avg.	1.3	0.8	0.6	0.7
Helps Reduce Air Pollution	2.0	Alphane	1.8	1.1	0.8	0.9
		Comp. Avg.	1.8	1.6	1.0	1.2
High Octane	1.8	Alphane	3.5	2.8	1.9	2.1
		Comp. Avg.	2.5	2.0	1.4	1.7
Provides Plenty of Power	1.6	Alphane	3.3	2.7	1.6	1.8
		Comp. Avg.	2.8	1.9	1.2	1.6
Well Known Brand	1.6	Alphane	3.7	3.7	2.6	2.8
		Comp. Avg.	4.1	3.8	2.8	3.1